PortlandNeighborhood'
Guide to the
Perfect Portland Weekend

Dana Speer
Lorri Ely
Angela Scott

Outskirts Press, Inc.
Denver, Colorado

PortlandNeighborhood's Guide to the Perfect Portland Weekend
All Rights Reserved.
Copyright © 2008 Dana Speer, Lorri Ely, Angela Scott
V3.5

Outskirts Press, Inc.
http://www.outskirtspress.com

ISBN: 978-1-4327-1630-1

Library of Congress Control Number: 2007940312

Outskirts Press and the "OP" logo are trademarks belonging to Outskirts Press, Inc.

PRINTED IN THE UNITED STATES OF AMERICA

Dedication

To the great city and people of Portland, Oregon.

Table of Contents

To the Reader

While coursing your way through the following pages as well as during any exploration of the unparalleled city of Portland, Oregon, be aware that you may augment the information contained in this book by visiting:

www.PortlandNeighborhood.com.

There you will find—broken down by many of the neighborhoods we name in the following itineraries—further advice, listings, offerings, and descriptions. In addition, the website comprehensively details points of interest like parks and libraries and matters of interest such as history and statistics. There you will even find several videos that capture much of the above to help enrich your discovery of one of the finest, most multifaceted cities on the planet.

Introduction

First of all, to know Portland is to know that it is not just a city. Portland is a culture. We may not always be on the same page, but let's just say that together we're strong on narrative. And ultimately the story is about America, the way it used to be—before every corner block in every city offered the same three restaurants, before driving out of one town and into another became an indistinguishable experience, before the illusion of choice became mistaken for free enterprise, fair trade, and a market worth your interaction.

But this book isn't a political manifesto. It's a celebration. It's an exaltation of a special population bound together to rejoice in difference. In the process, Portland couldn't help but be set apart. The purpose of this book then is simply to share the ways in which the unique and special are manifested within Portland's distinct and inimitable neighborhoods, their businesses, and their people.

Rather than simply list and review establishments, however, we thought you might find yourself better able to navigate the abundant options available in our fine burg of over four-score individually styled neighborhoods if we devised a pattern of approach. In other words, we've attempted to make Portland more mentally accessible, possible to wrap your mind around, by conceiving every chapter as representing a different hypothetical weekend, each with its own theme.

So, depending on your interests, you can access Portland tailor made. If you're the active type forever with hiking boots on your feet and a bike between your legs, there's a chapter just for you. If you're the one who can never get enough of the ballpark and your favorite sport, from the stands of course, we've composed a weekend for you too. Those with families, those looking to commune with nature and wildlife, those seeking culture and class to the romantics just seeking a kiss, those wanting to drop a couple dimes on shopping to those who are having to pinch every penny—yes, there's a chapter weekend for each of you. And of course, if you contain multitudes and more than one category applies to your types of interests, all the ideas are there to mix and match for your perfect Portland itinerary.

We welcome you to enjoy your time here. As both a location and a lifestyle, Portland's a trip!

Romantic Weekend

Eastbank Esplanade

W hat's a Bogie and Bergman goodbye without the tarmac? Robert Redford washes Meryl Streep's hair in a bathroom—we have entertainment. He washes it in the middle of the African wilderness—we have permanence. And we don't really need to be reminded where John Cusack and his boombox were, do we?

Interesting thing is, celluloid memories aren't the only ones where location is paramount. Take even the most casual of strolls down memory lane, and you'll see that highlights from your own romantic past will include a presumably brief roster of those present at the moment, perhaps a large list of feelings and emotions elicited, and last, but certainly not least, the setting. Like the vows that may or may not have accompanied, for better or worse the setting completed your romantic picture and to this day locates your romantic memory.

Some moments are fun to leave to chance, serendipity, and fate. More often than one typically seizes, however, there is an opportunity to take a joyride in the director's chair. And Portland, with its grand beauty as well as social and cultural vibe that allow for a nearly endless array of romantic activity options, is nothing less than the perfect place to go on location.

So if Hollywood cares enough to make its celluloid memories of romance indelible, shouldn't you? After all, it's your story. Besides, we've done all the scouting.

FRIDAY

6:00 PM

QUICK PEEK

The first time you see the skyline of downtown Portland is something you don't forget. It can literally alter any direction you thought you were heading. The opportunity to share that experience with the one you love will be indescribable and should therefore not be missed. So the vantage point available at the Vera Katz Eastbank Esplanade is the perfect place to get an eyeful of the adventure that awaits you while, if you so desire, getting in a stroll worthy of movie music.

The Eastbank Esplanade (SE Water Avenue & SE Hawthorne Blvd) offers 1.5 miles of riverfront walking, biking, or benches for sitting with panoramic views of downtown across the scenic Willamette River. Enter the experience at whichever level of activity you wish and simply enjoy the scene as well as each other.

7:00 PM

GET A ROOM!

If an explanation is necessary as to why the choice of hotel for a romantic getaway is of vital importance, perhaps you're looking for a different chapter. If, however, you've turned to the right page, the following is a sample of the range in romantic hotel options Portland has to offer.

Wine is often perfectly paired with romance, and the Hotel Vintage Plaza (422 SW Broadway; 800–263–2305) celebrates that marriage with each room dedicated to a different Oregon winery. Recognized by *Travel & Leisure* as one of the "500 Best Hotels in the World" and centrally located to the arts, shopping, and waterfront, the Hotel Vintage Plaza offers Starlight rooms with solarium-style windows angled for sweeping views of the night sky and downtown, two-story rooms, and balcony spa guestrooms with private, two-person hot tubs located on each veranda.

Perhaps a cozy bed and breakfast is your romantic speed. The Irvington neighborhood on Portland's northeast side boasts at least two B&Bs within convenient distance to a long strip of outdoor stroll shopping along lower northeast Broadway as well as Lloyd Center Mall where you might want to try an arm-in-arm twirl or two on the indoor ice-skating rink. Built in 1905 and listed on the National Register of Historic Places not to mention its listing as one of the Best Places to Kiss, the Queen Anne mansion housing The Lion and the Rose Victorian Bed and Breakfast Inn (1810 NE 15th Avenue; 800–955–1647) has six rooms, each unique and included with its own bath. In addition, two full courses of breakfast greet you in the morning.

The second B&B, looking quite similar to its namesake on Pennsylvania Avenue, Portland's White House Bed and Breakfast (1914 NE 22nd Avenue; 800–272–7131) offers five guest rooms in its main house and three in the Carriage House, all with their own bath. Vegetarian breakfast is served, with hormone–free meats on the side if you prefer, observing the conventions of Slow Food ethos by candlelight.

(Slow Food is a non–profit educational organization begun in Italy in 1989, with Portland as its first American chapter in what has now grown to 130 nationwide. Along with an emphasis on sustainable and local, Slow Food U.S.A. attempts to enhance life quality by slowing down and appreciating the traditions of communal bread breaking at the table.)

To make baby feel like a star, Hotel deLuxe (729 SW 15th Ave; 866–895–2094) will keep the credits rolling. The theme of the hotel is the golden era of Hollywood, and the offer on the table is to treat you like a studio chief. The Marlene Dietrich Suite features an eight-foot circular bed, and amenities throughout the hotel include a pillow menu, a *spiritual* menu, and a "make it so" button for any extra pampering baby might require. Their Love Is In the Air package comes with chilled champagne, one-hour in room massage for two, rose petals, and candlelight. If baby prefers things a little more aerobic, the "Twisted Love" package comes with champagne, a game of Twister "sure to get the romantic juices flowing," and an intimacy kit with massage oil and other surprises.

For an ultra hip—and just wee bit naughty—getaway, the Jupiter Hotel in the neighborhood of Buckman (800 E. Burnside; 877–800–0004) offers sleek, stylish, simple modern rooms—and Room #117. Go behind this door, and you'll find Spartacus, the hotel's own adult store, offering toys and games for your playtime. Providing Love and Lust at the Jupiter, the hotel and Spartacus have teamed up to offer the Spartacus Leather's Naughty package and the Spartacus Leather's Nice Package.

Of course, if you're into sleek and modern without straps and clamps, there's always the couple's massage at Mana Massage (811 E Burnside, Suite 218; 503–232–MELT). Owned and operated by Jenni Jo McLaughlin who is the caliber of massage therapist invited on tour with such names as Faith Hill and Tim McGraw, Mana Massage is affiliated with the Jupiter hotel and conveniently located just across the street.

The Jupiter also comes complete with one of Portland's most popular music venues, the Doug Fir, in addition to a restaurant and bar. Concert packages are available as well and include your room, two tickets to the night's show, VIP passes, and two drinks on the house. Or of course you can always customize your weekend stay by listening to a bit of rock while you play with a bit of blue.

8:00 PM

LIP SMACKING GOOD

High-end modern or old fashioned traditional? If to you romantic dinner for two looks like candles and silky, billowy curtains hanging from the ceiling at odd angles with kicked up versions of Mediterranean dishes like gnocchi with black truffles and bacon wrapped sea scallops in an establishment considered by Gourmet Magazine as the, "most sophisticated, contemporary food in town," then Bluehour (250 NW 13th Avenue; 503–226–3394) will be a wonderfully sexy dining excursion.

At the other end of the romantic restaurant spectrum, Fish Grotto (1035 SW Stark; 503–226–4171) allows one the opportunity to go retro in romance to an atmosphere of dark wood, cozy tradition, and intimately arranged dining. Serving romantics for over a century with dishes like salmon and marionberry pinot noir sauce, this fine dining experience has also served as the perfect venue for a proposal of marriage, the story of which is near and dear.

10:30 PM

GROOVE AND GROG

After an amorous culinary adventure, some tunes are in order, and in Portland the late night music and dancing scene has a move for whatever mood you're in. For large scale, sweaty beats, head to the 15,000 square foot dance floor of Barracuda (9 NW 2nd Avenue; 503–228–6900). Or the rhythm can just do its thing as you and your partner cozy up behind one of the curtained cabanas upstairs.

Can't make up your mind if you're ready for a racing pulse just yet, then try the unique space comprised of the Crystal Ballroom, Lola's Room, and Ringlers (1332 W. Burnside; 503–225–0047). Part of the family of McMenamins restaurants, bars, hotels, and theaters that are a slice of Portland in themselves, each one distinct and inimitable, the Crystal, Lola's, and Ringlers offer three floors of choices. Popular touring acts play several nights a week on the Ballroom tier, which boasts a 90-year-old "floating" dance floor that literally moves in rhythm with the crowd, a sensation that is not to be missed. Beneath the Ballroom, Lola's Room is a smaller venue that offers live music and D.J. mixes. However, if you just feel like sharing a coffee cocktail and conversation before heading back to your hotel, you can mosey down to the bottom floor, Ringlers, and sidle up to the mosaic-lined bar or shoot a casual game of pool.

And finally, for a chance just to share a moment with your partner without having to pump it to electronica or even play pool, head to the jazz bar at Wilf's (800 NW 6th Avenue; 503–223–0070). Located at Portland's historic Union Station, Wilf's riffs on free live cool jazz at least every Friday and Saturday night so that all you and your date have to do is show up and snuggle tableside.

1:00 AM

BACK TO YOUR PLACE

This itinerary is up to you.

SATURDAY

9:00 AM

EVEN A FLAME NEEDS FUEL

Plus, those legs of yours just might need a stretch by now. So take a walk to probably the last place you're thinking about this weekend—Mom's house. Portland's version of your mom's kitchen is Mother's Bistro (212 SW Stark Street; 503–464–1122), and it is considered absolutely *the place* to have breakfast. Mother's is old world meets by-gone Americana meets sexy from décor to dinner. They feed you like Mom used to—except here Mom's food is amped. So you'll have to do a few extra stomach crunches when you get home, but dishes like the corn flake crusted French toast and the hold-the-phone-can't-talk-now biscuits and gravy make it worth any toll you'll pay at the gym.

However, if you chose a hotel located on the eastside of the Willamette River, another tremendous option is Francis (2338 NE Alberta Street; 503–288–8299). They make just about everything you can think of from scratch including the smoked salmon that they serve in a my-heart-just-skipped-an-unsafe-amount-of-beats homage to eggs Benedict. They also open at 7:00, so, if you rousted early and have some extra time on your hands, after breakfast you can stroll the unique and eclectic offerings that line the neighborhood renaissance that is northeast Alberta.

10:30 AM

JUICES FLOWING

Waterfront Bicycle Rentals (10 SW Ash, Suite 100; 503–227–1719) offers a wide range of bikes for rent, including hybrid, road, and even tandem, in a variety of brand names at rates beginning at one hour up to one day or by the week. Waterfront Bicycle Rentals is located very near the picturesque bike path that runs along Portland's downtown riverfront. So rent two bikes—or a tandem if you're a serious cycler—and ask the owners (another couple such as yourselves) to orient you along the bike path map. Depending on your level of cycling prowess and your desire for activity, a good 90 minute to two hour ride north along the path to the Steel Bridge, across the bridge to the east side of the Corridor to the Sellwood Bridge and then back again is a good workout with tremendous vantage points of the Willamette river and the city.

12:00 PM

CUE THE VIOLINS

Portland Spirit (110 SE Caruthers Street; 800–224–3901) offers lunch, dinner, and Sunday brunch cruises, Great Rivers of the Northwest Excursions, and jetboat rides along the Willamette. And if you keep your bike ride a little closer to its point of origin, at noon you may take a break and leave the bank of the river for the water itself. This lovely lunch cruise is available for sightseeing only, with an upgrade possible based on seating availability should you change your mind. Call ahead for reservations, and they'll be happy to have a bouquet of roses waiting for you to gift your surprised date as you set sail. And then simply sit back with a glass of wine on one of the decks and enjoy two hours of the best seats in the house with gorgeous views of the river and skyline.

3:00 PM

OBLIGATORY STROLL

What is it with romance and walking? In the movies, it's typically an excuse for a montage. And perhaps fulfilling the same function in real life, a stroll passes the time and gives us something else to do with our bodies that won't land us in the emergency room deadlocked, so-to-speak.

11

So, we've left a little buffer between the cruise and this activity so you may ride your bikes a little more if you desire. But after you return your bicycles, return yourselves to nearby RiverPlace. There you'll find the Little River Café (315 SW Montgomery Street, Suite 310; 503–227–2327), where you may certainly wish to treat yourselves to a scoop or more of ice cream. Then obviously, if you've been paying attention to the movie, it is now incumbent upon you to nibble away at your treat as you stroll along the eclectic shops of RiverPlace, enjoying the sights and sounds of the marina.

4:30 PM

LANDLUBBERS

Leaving the river behind now, you will nonetheless continue the arm-in-arm action along the Alberta Arts District. If you chose Francis for breakfast earlier in the morning, you saw some of Alberta but definitely not all. For a more comprehensive description of Alberta, refer to the chapter related to Portland shopping. But for purposes of this weekend, let's just say that the gentrification makeover happening there is legendary 'round these parts, and it's a highly recommended stop for any Portland getaway. Lovers specifically will enjoy the lengthy strolling op it provides, the seemingly endless fodder for art discussions, and the many eclectic, quintessential Portland shopping options. Stop in at, say, Mabel and Zora (1468 NE Alberta; 503–335–6169) for that perfect number for tonight's dinner. Drop by Tribute (1805 NE Alberta; 503–493–9520) to shop amongst their in-house skateboard apparel. And if painting a smile is in your plans, then a bouquet of flowers from the truly unique Origin Flowers should definitely be on your palette (1532 NE Alberta; 503–775–9599).

At any point when you're ready for a rest, many, many options await you, but, if the weather is cooperating, a visit to the spectacular patio of the Tin Shed (1438 NE Alberta; 503–288–6966) is way in order. Grab a drink and an appetizer if you've got an appetite and snuggle up on a bench in the garden portion of the outdoor seating area or next to the fireplace under the patio's cover if the garden is a wee damp or cool.

6:00 PM

REFRESH BUTTON

Take this time to do whatever your heart tells you to be able to regroup for the evening ahead.

OR...

...if the bike ride doesn't sound like the kind of workout you had in mind for a romantic weekend, an alternate plan could include an arm-in-arm visit to the Cultural District of Downtown Portland. There you can experience together the Portland Art Museum (1219 SW Park Avenue; 503–226–2811) with a collection that ranges from American, Asian, and European through Native American and contemporary.

Then, conveniently located just across the street from the art museum, is the Oregon Historical Society (1200 SW Park Avenue; 503–222–1741) where you'll have the

13

opportunity to learn even more about your new adopted romantic home.

Bisecting the Cultural District is a lushly landscaped park that extends for six city blocks and boasts a grandiose stand of Dutch Elm trees. This is your cue to take yet another halcyon stroll with your favorite co-star.

Afterward, enjoy a ride on any number of daily cruises on the Willamette or the Columbia rivers operated by Portland Spirit.

Following the cruise—or in lieu of the cruise depending on weather and time—a trip to the Willamette Valley wine country is strongly recommended. Call 503–646–2985 or visit their website listed at the end of this chapter for a list of vineyards and tours. Then snuggle in the back of a limousine as your chauffeur escorts you through the picturesque countryside to wineries both large and boutique.

7:30 PM

ROMANTIC RED CARPET

Your carriage awaits, so just sit back and be treated like the romantic royalty you know you are. Golden Times Carriage Service (503–666–4647) will pick you up in a horse drawn carriage and escort you through downtown for a half-hour, hour, or longer. All you need to do is bring a bottle of wine and an insatiable appetite for special moments.

8:30 PM

A DINING ROOM WITH A VIEW

Perhaps the swept-from-your-feet, tingly nature of a grand sight resonates with the swooning butterflies in your belly. And perhaps a psychologist could offer further insights. But you're here to enjoy yourself, and we're too far on a mission to turn back and dissertate now. So let's just say we're pretty sure that any recipe for romance should call for dinner and a view. And those ingredients, bar none, can be found at Portland City Grill (111 SW 5th Avenue; 503-450-0030), which offers the very best romantic views of the city, not to mention the competition below.

Located on the 30th floor of the Bancorp Tower, the restaurant doesn't dish only the view. It also offers fine dining in the form of steak, seafood, and sushi. Arrive early for your reservation and take a seat in the piano bar where you can listen to live, lilting tones as you enjoy a pre-dinner cocktail and a slightly different, but just as spectacular, perspective on the stunning views available.

10:30 PM

JUST DESSERTS

The necessity of the arm-in-arm stroll for two has well been established in this chapter. The requisite nature of a well timed post-dinner walk has not been discussed but is no less imperative for the romantically inclined, especially if you're hell bent on delicious sin.

15

On the northwest side of the city, Nob Hill's 23rd Avenue is lined in charming fashion with Victorian and craftsman style homes interspersed with more modern buildings. And most house everything from eclectic shops to bars and coffee houses. Many of the street's establishments will be closed at this time of night, but several will still be open, and there will likely yet be at least some street activity. Window shop, pop into any place that draws the eye, but your destination, just so you know, is Papa Haydn (701 NW 23rd Avenue; 503–228–7317).

Named after an 18th century Viennese composer who was kind and fatherly, and of course to capture the renown of Viennese pastry, Papa Haydn is literally a Portland household name that is absolutely synonymous with the best homemade dessert in town. Even at this time of night, there is such a frenzied Portland appetite for Papa Haydn's treats that there will probably be a buzz, and you might have to wait to be seated. And in case you're thinking this is some dive diner that just figured its way around sugar, think again. Papa Haydn is fine dining with décor to match. So wait for your table, order as much as you like—but only one fork—and dig into a classy blast. Or take it to go, again with only one fork, and follow the same directions.

Another option further still, if you find yourselves too full from dinner to think of another bite, one of the coziest, coolest bars in town for an after dinner, quiet cocktail is the Driftwood Room located at the Hotel deLuxe (729 SW 15th Avenue; 866–895–2094). Dark and sophisticated, the Driftwood Room offers the kind of sultry privacy and warmth at the back of your throat that is pure old Hollywood and destined to etch yet another reel into your memory.

16

SUNDAY

9:00 AM

BREAKFAST ON A BLANKET

Part of what makes romance so inspiring is not just that there is another taking up space in our lives, but that our lives are taking up new space. Everything is suddenly novel, remarkably original and innovative—even breakfast if we take a moment to pimp it. Ken's Artisan Bakery (338 NW 21st Avenue; 503–248–2202) is the Portland bomb when it comes to daily fresh baked goods, and their pizza business located on the east side has even gotten the attention of The Food Network. Stop by and load up on breakfast picnic supplies from their huge variety of pastry, bread, croissants, tarts, and more. Then take your bounty to the world famous International Rose Test Garden at the peak of Washington Park (400 SW Kingston Avenue; 503–823–3636) and smell for yourself why Portland is called the City of Roses.

The official testing site for the All-America Rose Selection, the International Rose Test Garden is row after row of rose bushes, hundreds of varieties, thousands of blossoms. It is quite simply a garden the likes of which few have witnessed. In addition, as it is perched atop the city's west hills, the garden boasts one of the most breathtaking natural views of Portland available. Grab one of the picnic tables above the garden or drape a blanket on the grass of the garden's amphitheatre and enjoy a breakfast dished with a slice of Portland bliss.

11:00 AM

SPLENDOR IN THE GARDEN

When you've wiped your lips of the last picnic morsels, you won't have to go far for the rest of your morning treat. Right there at the top of Washington Park, nearly a stone's throw from where you picnicked, is the Japanese Garden (611 SW Kingston Avenue; 503–223–1321). Carefully landscaped to resonate harmony and present an opportunity for serenity and meditation, the garden is actually comprised of five distinct garden styles: the Strolling Pond Garden, Tea Garden, Natural Garden, Flat Garden, and a Sand and Stone Garden. This is of course another opportunity to stroll, but this time the embrace is sheer tranquility.

1:30 PM

FEELING KINKY?

Well, get over it as the professionals move their mojo along the kinks, cricks, and strains in your neck and back during a couple's massage. And just to increase the serious potential for relaxation, again you won't have to go far.

Located near the base of Washington Park is the beginning of Nob Hill's 23rd Avenue where you may have spent the latter part of the previous evening digging into devilish desserts. Now this street is once again the gateway to indulgence. This time, however, you will completely pamper yourselves in one of Portland's premiere day spas, Dosha Salon Spa (2281 NW Glisan; 503–228–8280) or Equilibria Massage and Bodywork (1536 NW 23rd Avenue;

503–221–2155), simply the perfect places to have knots removed as bonds grow even tighter.

2:30 PM

AFTERNOON DELIGHT

Basking in the inevitable post-massage glow, take a leisurely stroll down NW 23rd Avenue toward your lunchtime destination. At this time on a Sunday, the area will most likely be happening. Take it at your own pace and, if you're up to it, enjoy the utterly fabulous shopping available, more details on which can be found in the Shopping Weekend chapter. Directly or eventually, you decide, make your way two blocks east toward the fine cuisine of the Pacific Northwest as conceived and dished by Wildwood and executive chef, Dustin Clark (1221 NW 21st Avenue; 503–248–9663). There you might sample from one another's plates such morsels as confit of Draper Valley chicken leg, Willapa Bay oyster salad, or even a kicked up take on a burger or pizza.

However, if your massage has rendered you feeling like something a little more casual—as well as your hair a manipulated mess—be aware that, around the corner from 23rd Avenue on Kearney, not even a block, are the handcrafted ales and yummy dishes from salmon to burgers of Laurelwood Public House (2327 NW Kearney; 503–228–5553).

Both restaurants offer outdoor seating, so melt back in your chair and sip a brew or glass of wine, reflect over the mental movie you and your romantic partner just shot on the perfect location and start planning the sequel.

The Skinny

Lay Your Head

Hotel deLuxe 729 SW 15th Avenue; 866–895–2094;
www.hoteldeluxeportland.com
Hotel Vintage Plaza 422 SW Broadway; 800–263–2305;
www.vintageplaza.com
Jupiter Hotel 800 E. Burnside; 877–800–0004;
www.jupiterhotel.com
The Lion and the Rose Victorian Bed and Breakfast Inn
1810 NE 15th Avenue; 800–955–1647; www.lionrose.com
White House Bed and Breakfast 1914 NE 22nd Avenue;
800–272–7131; www.portlandswhitehouse.com

Cool Your Heels

Barracuda 9 NW 2nd Avenue; 503–228–6900;
www.cegportland.com
Bluehour 250 NW 13th Avenue; 503–226–3394;
www.bluehouronline.com
Crystal Ballroom, Lola's Room, and **Ringlers** 1332 W.
Burnside; 503–225–0047, www.mcmenamins.com
Driftwood Room 729 SW 15th Avenue; 866–895–2094;
www.hoteldeluxeportland.com

Fish Grotto 1035 SW Stark; 503–226–4171; www.fishgrotto.com

Francis 2338 NE Alberta Street; 503–288–8299; www.francisrestaurant.com

Ken's Artisan Bakery 338 NW 21st Avenue; 503–248–2202; www.kensartisan.com

Laurelwood Public House 2327 NW Kearney Street; 503–228–5553; www.laurelwoodbrewpub.com

Little River Café 315 SW Montgomery Street, Suite 310; 503–227–2327

Mother's Bistro 212 SW Stark Street; 503–464–1122; www.mothersbistro.com

Papa Haydn 701 NW 23rd Avenue; 503–228–7317; www.papahaydn.com

Portland City Grill 111 SW 5th Avenue; 503–450–0030; www.portlandcitygrill.com

Tin Shed 1438 NE Alberta; 503–288–6966; www.tinshedgardencafe.com

Wildwood 1221 NW 21st Avenue; 503–248–9663; www.wildwoodrestaurant.com

Wilf's 800 NW 6th Avenue; 503–223–0070; www.wilfsrestaurant.com

Actions Speak Louder Than Words

International Rose Test Garden 400 SW Kingston Avenue; 503–823–3636; www.portlandonline.com

Japanese Garden 611 SW Kingston Avenue; 503–223–1321; www.japanesegarden.com

Oregon Historical Society 1200 SW Park Avenue; 503–222–1741; www.ohs.org

Portland Art Museum 1219 SW Park Avenue; 503–226–2811; www.portlandartmuseum.org

Portland Spirit 110 SE Caruthers Street; 800–224–3901;

www.portlandspirit.com
Vera Katz Eastbank Esplanade SE Water Avenue & SE Hawthorne Blvd; www.40mileloop.org
Willamette Valley Wine Country 503–646–2985; www.willamettewines.com

Get It In Gear

Mabel and Zora 1468 NE Alberta; 503–335–6169; www.mabelandzora.com
Origin Flowers 1532 NE Alberta; 503–775–9599; www.originflowers.com
Tribute 1805 NE Alberta; 503–493–9520
Waterfront Bicycle Rentals 10 SW Ash, Suite 100; 503–227–1719; www.waterfrontbikes.net

It's All About You

Dosha Salon Spa 2281 NW Glisan; 503–228–8280; www.dosha.org
Equilibria Massage and Bodywork 1536 NW 23rd Avenue; 503–221–2155; www.equilibriamassage.com
Golden Times Carriage Service 503–666–4647
Mana Massage 811 E Burnside, Suite 218; 503–232–MELT; www.manamassage.us

Check Under the 'Hood

Alberta Arts District
www.portlandneighborhood.com/alberta–street.html

Buckman
www.portlandneighborhood.com/buckman.html

Downtown
www.portlandneighborhood.com/downtown–portland.html

Irvington
www.portlandneighborhood.com/irvington.html

Nob Hill
www.portlandneighborhood.com/nobhill.html

Active Weekend

Jetboat, Willamette River

M uch like a child's repetitive tap on your arm that is sensed but not quite registered when you're busy, something about Portland will occur to you, perhaps peripherally but immediately, upon arrival. It may take a moment to put your finger on, but it's that, "Toto, we're not in Cookie-Cutter anymore" sensation that won't be denied. Bumper stickers proclaim, "Keep Portland Weird." A local radio station repeatedly announces, "It's different here." And the plain fact of the matter is it is.

Don't fret however. It's not like we're separatists or elitists. We're not crazy, commie, or compound bound. We just tend to do things a little differently. An entire description of the Portland culture and reasons for its being are another book or even volume box set. But for purposes of this chapter, we'll just say that this is the kind of place where a corporate type might skateboard to work, a trip to REI is a hot Saturday night, and biking is a fevered community mantra in which cyclists demand their streets, organizing rides that traverse every bridge, that take place at night in costume, that take place at night in birthday costume. Oh yeah.

And really, we can't be blamed for our joyful enthusiasm for all things active. Can we help it that nature has provided us with our own backyard playground? Can we help it that we find ourselves inspired to let our bodies do what comes naturally and express themselves in all manner of sport? Nay. But we are gleefully culpable in spreading the contagion.

So look at it this way. You want to enjoy the weekend. We're always at some form of recess. Welcome to our sandbox. We're not always well behaved, but we play nicely.

FRIDAY

6:00 PM

JUMP START

Over the eons this area has not been without its pressure points to be sure. To wit, sitting on the eastern edge of Portland is one of only two extinct volcanoes within city limits in the entire United States. The other is a couple hours away in Bend, Oregon. But right here in Portland, Mt. Tabor (SE 60th and SE Salmon St.) offers a gentle hike to its relatively low summit and is a perfect way to debug your travel jitters and begin the active weekend before you. Once at the top, there are stunning views of the city, downtown in the distance and, depending on how long it takes you to summit, an approaching sunset. (As mentioned in other chapters, summers in Portland allow for at least a few rays of daylight as late as 10:00.)

Once you've reached the peak, pull up a bench and enjoy a free and delicious snack of eye candy.

8:00 PM

HIKE, HUNT, AND GATHER

Hunting for a place to eat is a serious matter, and you're in full on active mojo mode, so we'll keep you moving. At the base of Mt. Tabor you'll find Hawthorne Boulevard. One of Portland's liveliest and most popular destination neighborhoods is the Hawthorne District, which runs approximately between the blocks of 55th and 11th Avenues on Hawthorne Boulevard. Just about anything one may desire out of an evening's entertainment is available along these blocks. Enjoy a stroll at whatever pace you desire and explore the quirky fun that is Hawthorne.

As you make your way, you may find a restaurant or bar or even brewpub movie theater (Bagdad Theater and Pub; 3702 SE Hawthorne; 503–236–9234) that calls to you louder, but for the very best Indian food this side of the Ganges with a gourmet flourish, knockout cocktails, and a cozy atmosphere, head to Bombay Cricket Club (1925 SE Hawthorne; 503–231–0740).

10:00 PM

PINHEAD

For unfathomable reasons, fitness buffs are not typically associated with bowling. But that's an outrage. Few other sports besides those found in pubs and on the golf course possess such raw, inherent challenges. After all, can you imagine a runner trying to compete with that much beer in their system? But bowlers do it all the time. So, if you think you might like to stay active at this time of night, head over to what is probably the swankiest bowling alley you've ever worn funny shoes in, Grand Central Restaurant and Bowling Lounge (839 SE Morrison; 503-236-BOWL).

As the name of the joint might imply, this ain't no joint. Couches await you at each alley instead of the typical Formica hard-ass. Each lane is punctuated with its own giant HD projection screen, and there is even a VIP area with its own private seating, lanes, and optional bar. And though you're probably far more interested in knocking down pins than knocking back more vittles, the restaurant serves things like pear and gorgonzola salad and coconut prawns, and the bar/lounge areas are sleek and attractive.

Flashing fancy moves that render elements of the bowling vernacular such as "alley" and "gutter" nearly out of place, Grand Central will roll ya' till 2:30 on Fridays. So you should have more than enough time to get back in touch with your inner Dudeness.

12:30 AM

NO DICE

Unlike its namesake location, Hotel Monaco Portland (506 SW Washington St.; 888–207–2201) won't have you playing the casino, but you'll have royal access to the activities ahead. And though we're pretty much gonna keep you in a perpetual state of deodorant deficiency, if you're an active type cranked on sweating, chances are good you'll want to get in an extra workout. Fitting that bill, the Hotel Monaco has its own fitness room and is located just a few blocks from the more extensive inventory of equipment as well as pool and Jacuzzi available at the downtown location of 24-Hour Fitness (1407 SW 4th Avenue; 503–224–2233). There, free (up to) seven-day guest passes are available if you call for a set-up appointment in advance.

If, however, an active weekend to you means well deserved relaxation during your downtime, the Hotel Monaco
is a charming affair with attractive rooms and suites and
plenty of amenities such as in room spa services to help
you put your feet up after they've literally been running all
day.

SATURDAY

8:00 AM

TOUR DE FRESH

In keeping with the spirit of the morning ahead, head to St.
Honore' Boulangerie (2335 NW Thurman; 503–445–4342)
where during the Tour de France it is standing room only
for Portland's bike crazed population. Here you may enjoy
fresh French homemade breads, croissants, pastries, quiche,
soup, sandwiches—and a true morning taste of classic Portland.

9:00 AM

GEARED UP

Located just down the street from the Boulangerie is The
Fat Tire Farm (2714 NW Thurman; 503–222–3276), the
perfect place to catch a ride, so-to-speak. They carry both
mountain and road bicycles and certainly everything you
need for the coming excursion. They can even advise with
regard to routes, and they stock maps that will direct you to

nearby firelanes where you can release that mountain biking action you've been revving. In fact, the street where Fat Tire Farm is located leads to the trailhead for Leif Erikson Drive Trail, where many of the firelanes intersect. So let the Farm suit you up and head you out.

9:30 AM

SPINNING YOUR WHEELS

The largest natural forest park within city limits in the country, Forest Park (NW 29th Avenue and Upshur to Newberry Road; 503–823–PLAY) offers a spectacular, winding firelane system that easily links up with Portland's 40-Mile Loop. Riding in the park is restricted only to firelanes, but they are extensive and plentiful. Then, depending on the type of ride you're up for, you may stay within the park or, for a much longer ride, take the 40-Mile Loop and head all the way to Gresham on Portland's southeast side or Troutdale on its northeast. If you choose to take on the whole loop, you'll have the opportunity to ride along both the Willamette River running directly through Portland as well as the Columbia, which flows along the city's north side. Be aware though that, as exhaustively extensive as the Loop is, there yet remain a few gaps, so visit their website, listed at the end of this chapter, for a map of those gaps. Then supplement with other city maps to navigate around patches where the Loop still requires more construction, and/or follow the signs.

Side Note: As you meander your way through the park, by foot or by bike, you may find yourself nearing the towering gothic arches of the suspension bridge leading to the

St. Johns neighborhood. Dating back to 1865, St. Johns was originally settled independently of Portland and still boasts a main street that, though certainly not reminiscent of its earliest days, remains a step back in time and a side trip definitely worth a jaunt over the bridge.

So whether you take most of the day to explore the 40– Mile Loop or just a few hours to enjoy Forest Park and its numerous mountain biking firelanes is up to you. The timing of the next few options on your day is therefore very flexible.

1:00 PM

REST AND RETRIEVE

The Lucky Labrador Beer Hall (1945 NW Quimby; 503–517–4352) and its affection for Portland bike culture is only matched by its love for dogs. So, if after a demanding ride you feel like tipping back a well-earned homemade brew and chowing down on a sandwich, salad, or bento in a cavernous warehouse environment that also devoutly displays the Tour de France on a television that is otherwise off and hidden from view, then hit the Lucky Lab.

This is not a tourist destination. This is a dog hair on the floor mats kind of place. This is smiles, good times, good beer, good bento with, likely, several others who arrived either on two wheels or four legs. This is Portland.

2:00 PM

CARDIAC PUMP

After you've had a chance to catch your breath, get ready to go breathless once again. First, take a leisurely ride through downtown via the safest route available. For a map of bike lanes and shared roadways, visit:

www.portlandonline.com/transportation

Then, cross over the river to the city's east side and head to Willamette Jetboat Excursions (1945 SE Water Avenue; 888–JETBOAT) because we've come to the conclusion that when someone else is offering to get your heart pumping—and it's legal—you gotta jump on that.

So, depending on the time of year, time of day, and your energy level, you have a choice of one or two-hour rides that mix both exhilarating speeds with slower paced sightseeing explorations of the river, its bridges, and its wildlife. Have a blast!

4:00 PM

SECOND CHANCES

If you chose to stay within Forest Park earlier, here's another chance to explore a bit of the 40-Mile Loop before your next adventure. The jetboat company is located very near the section of the Loop called the Vera Katz Eastbank Esplanade (SE Water Avenue & SE Hawthorne Boulevard). This part of the Loop offers extraordinary views of the river as well as downtown and is a swift, easy ride. And of course, time permitting, you have the option to continue along the Loop as far as you like. But pace yourself to be fit and ready for the next excursion as well as the ride across the river to get to it.

6:00 PM

RIDE OFF INTO THE SUNSET

Yes, that's right. We know what time it is. But from May through September primarily, every night at 6:00 sharp Portland Kayak Company (RiverPlace Marina; 503–229–0551) offers a sunset tour that even the kayaking novice can enjoy. On this excursion, you'll circumnavigate Ross Island in the Willamette River, passing a Blue Heron rookery and maybe even nabbing a glimpse of one of our area's bald eagles. And you'll have a fish's eye view of the Portland skyline on the way back.

9:00 PM

GONE FISHING

Any active weekender worth his or her REI dividends should certainly love the chance to catch their own dinner. At Blue Fin Sushi (1988 SW Broadway; 503–274–7922) patrons can enjoy the full experience of fishing as-it-were for their own sushi as it passes in front of them on a conveyor belt. All your favorites are there. But it's up to you to snare 'em.

10:30 PM

ONE SMALL STEP FOR MAN

At Voodoo Doughnut (22 SW 3rd Avenue; 503–241–4704), Portland's highly quirky, 24-hour establishment where "the magic is in the hole," the selection of doughnuts is inventive and highly imaginative. (Some were apparently a little too imaginative, like the NyQuil glazed doughnut, currently unavailable.)

Sample a Portland Crème, a raised doughnut filled with crème and covered in chocolate with two eyes, or a Neapolitan doughnut filled with vanilla frosting and strawberry Quick powder. Or try the bacon wrapped maple bar. Really. They even have vegan doughnuts and still others with R-rated titles that we'd just have too much fun listing here to be succinct.

But today you expended a hero's quotient of energy, so you deserve a dessert fit for an astronaut. So go ahead, Major Tom, order the Mango Tango doughnut covered with, you guessed it, Tang. Sure, it may not re-supply you with NASA-sized energy, but the sugar crash should help you sleep, and you need your rest for the day ahead.

SUNDAY

8:00 AM

ASSUME THE POSITION

For a very healthy, active, on-the-go breakfast, a perfect option is the Blooming Lotus Café (925 NW Davis; 503–228–0048). Part of the healing and renewal center that is Yoga in the Pearl, the Blooming Lotus offers kicked up vegetarian options like a breakfast parfait of granola, fruit, and nut crème as well as pate made from pumpkin seeds. Take your time with one of the breakfast selections or just grab a custom made smoothie and juice up for the coming action.

9:00 AM

BLAZING SADDLES

Is that an engine between your legs, or are you just happy to be here? S K Watercraft (3307 NE Marine Dr.; 503–284–6447) has all the equipment you need to jet ski on the Columbia and Willamette rivers. They also offer a short demonstration concerning the use and safety features of the vehicle before you hit the water. Their stock of jet skis are all 3-seaters, so, depending on the number in your party, you may need only one. (Reservations are recommended.)

12:30 PM

CAPTAIN'S NEST

If you chose to ride the Columbia, the most spectacular view of the river from a restaurant on the Portland side is to be found at Salty's on the Columbia (3839 NE Marine Dr.; 503–288–4444). As they also boast an extensive brunch seafood buffet, this is a great opportunity for you just to relax on one of the outdoor decks and look out over the expanse that you just sported your way through while grabbing a tasty bite and sipping on a well-deserved, handmade brunch Bloody.

2:00 PM

WHAT IS THAT SMELL?!

This is where that free membership to 24-Hour Fitness and a little thing called a shower can come in handy if you're feeling a little less than fresh after your dip in the river.

3:00 PM

GREAT UNDERSTANDING

Your feet have done a yeoman's job for you. Now it's your turn to pay them back. The Barefoot Sage (1844 SE Hawthorne; 503–239–7116) is a unique Portland spa devoted one hundred percent to feet, our oft-forgot foundations. Offering foot massage and therapies, the goal is to provide benefit to your mind and body—through your feet. All you've gotta do is put 'em up, sip a cup from their large menu of tea and drink in sheer bliss.

And any other sore muscles you're going to remember Portland by, well, you're welcome.

Important Side Note: Throughout the year, as alluded to during discussion of the naked bike ride (503–542–6900) in the introduction to this chapter, Portland offers several quirky outdoor activities. These include but are certainly not limited to such enterprises as adult soapbox racing (503–493–WINK) and skateboarding underneath the east side of Burnside Bridge where the city has looked the other way as its citizens fashioned for themselves their own urban skate park. A large skateboard park is also less clandestinely available in St. Johns at Pier Park. Visit the websites listed at the end of this chapter for more locations and ideas. Also, it should be noted that only 50 miles from Portland is Mt. Hood where, during the winter months, skiing and snowboarding are easily accessible. Hood River is also just a similar distance away and offers one of the world's premiere wind surfing destinations. And if you're a runner, right here the Portland Marathon (503–226–1111) is an annual high-octane bash.

The Skinny

Lay Your Head

Hotel Monaco Portland 506 SW Washington St.; 888–207–2201; www.monaco–portland.com

Cool Your Heels

Bagdad Theater and Pub 3702 SE Hawthorne; 503–236–9234; www.mcmenamins.com
Blooming Lotus Café 925 NW Davis; 503–228–0048; www.blpdx.com
Blue Fin Sushi 1988 SW Broadway; 503–274–7922
Bombay Cricket Club 1925 SE Hawthorne; 503–231–0740; www.bombaycricketclubrestaurant.com
Lucky Labrador Beer Hall 1945 NW Quimby; 503–517–4352; www.luckylab.com
Salty's on the Columbia 3839 NE Marine Dr.; 503–288–4444; www.saltys.com
St. Honore' Boulangerie 2335 NW Thurman; 503–445–4342; www.sainthonorebakery.com
Voodoo Doughnut 22 SW 3rd Avenue; 503–241–4704; www.voodoodoughnut.com

Actions Speak Louder Than Words

24-Hour Fitness 1407 SW 4th Avenue; 503–224–2233; www.24hourfitness.com

40-Mile Loop www.40mileloop.org

Adult Soapbox Racing 503–493–WINK; www.soapboxracer.com

Forest Park NW 29th Avenue and Upshur to Newberry Road; 503–823–PLAY; www.portlandonline.com/parks; www.greentrailsmaps.com

Grand Central Restaurant and Bowling Lounge 839 SE Morrison; 503-236-BOWL; www.thegrandcentralbowl.com

Mt. Tabor SE 60th and SE Salmon St.; 503–823–PLAY; www.portlandonline.com/parks

Naked Bike Ride 503–542–6900; www.shift2bikes.org/pedalpalooza

Portland Marathon 503–226–1111; www.portlandmarathon.org

Vera Katz Eastbank Esplanade SE Water Avenue & SE Hawthorne Boulevard; www.40mileloop.org

Willamette Jetboat Excursions 1945 SE Water Avenue; 888–JETBOAT; www.willamettejet.com

Get It In Gear

The Fat Tire Farm 2714 NW Thurman; 503–222–3276; www.fattirefarm.com

Portland Kayak Company RiverPlace Marina; 503–229–0551; www.portlandrivercompany.com

S K Watercraft 3307 NE Marine Dr.; 503–284–6447; www.sknorthwest.com

It's All About You

The Barefoot Sage 1844 SE Hawthorne; 503–239–7116; www.thebarefootsage.com

Check Under the 'Hood

Downtown
www.portlandneighborhood.com/downtown–portland.html

Hawthorne
www.portlandneighborhood.com/hawthorne.html

Pearl District
www.portlandneighborhood.com/pearldistrict.html

Richmond
www.portlandneighborhood.com/richmond.html

St. Johns
www.portlandneighborhood.com/stjohns.html

Highbrow Weekend

Portland's Classical Chinese Garden

M uch is said in this book about the state of Portland culture, but what about the state of culture in Portland? Culture with a capital "C"—you know the one. For some, that's exactly what is passed on the way to a good time. But for others, it's inspiration. It's hair on the back of your neck gone squirrelly. It's a damn good cry.

From touring Broadway shows and several of our own nationally acclaimed in-house theatre, ballet, and opera companies to a vibrant film community and regular public lecture series on science, literature, and more, Portland is nothing less than a cultural barn burner. We then stir that up with a highly competitive culinary landscape spiced with more than a dash of James Beard Award winning chefs and a music scene that is actually a scene.

So cue the violins and grab the Kleenex. Portland's got the goose bumps.

FRIDAY

6:00 PM

CENTER STAGE

Located in the very heart of Downtown Portland, The Heathman Hotel (1001 SW Broadway at Salmon; 800–551–0011) will be this weekend's perfect gateway hotel to Portland's Cultural District. The Heathman is located within very close walking distance to the three grand theatre buildings that comprise the Portland Center for the Per-

47

forming Arts and the very best that the Portland film community has to offer in addition to several other play and concert venues, museums, galleries, and even shopping.

Named by *Travel & Leisure* as one of the "500 Best Hotels in the World," The Heathman offers luxury with its own Art of Sleep bed menu, a pillow menu, and stay packages with names like "Museum," "Gourmet," "King or Queen for a Day," and even "Shop Till You Drop," wherein you have access to a personal shopper and, by appointment, early store hours at nearby Nordstrom. The hotel boasts a bar and restaurant featuring the winner of the 2001 James Beard Award for Excellence, Executive Chef Phillipe Boulot, in addition to its own art collection with works by Claude Galle and Andy Warhol.

7:00 PM

LIGHTS, CAMERA, ACTION!

You just got to town, so chances are you want to engage in an activity that is stimulating and thought provoking without being stressfully structured. In case your flight was delayed or you just want to relax in your room for a few moments longer than the itinerary might allow, tickets to a Broadway show right now might be more of a burden than a promise of a lovely night on the town. For that reason, we are suggesting an approximate time frame for any one of Portland's fine art film venues.

The Northwest Film Center (1219 SW Park Avenue; 503–221–1156) is a component of the Portland Art Museum that provides education, exhibition, and outreach. The

Outreach Program offers opportunities and support for media artists while the School of Film includes a curriculum in filmmaking, video production, and animation.

For your purposes this weekend, however, the Northwest Film Center is all about an incredibly extensive exhibition program that covers foreign, classic, experimental, and independent films. Screenings typically take place at the Whitsell Auditorium, located in the Portland Art Museum which, by the way, is extremely close to your hotel. The Northwest Film Center also plays host to unique rooftop screenings during the summer and an assortment of festivals, including the prestigious Portland International Film Festival, which screen at various locations.

You can typically count on Fridays at 7:00 for screening times at the Film Center's Whitsell Auditorium, but should that not be the case during your particular visit and/or you would like to have a further selection of art films to choose from, the following movie houses are exceedingly safe bets for some of the finest films screening in the entire country.

With a longstanding, popular tradition of fine film exhibition, Cinema 21 in Nob Hill (616 NW 21st Avenue; 503–223–4515) offers independent art house fare in a historic venue dating back to 1926.

A magnet for independent and revival films, Clinton Street Theater (2522 SE Clinton; 503–238–8899) has been a fixture of the Richmond neighborhood since 1915 and offers home brewed beer and food during the show.

Like Northwest Film Center, the Hollywood Theatre (4122 NE Sandy; 503–281–4215) also has its own education and support programs for filmmakers, and it exhibits independent, foreign, and classic movies in its 20's era theatre.

Created by longtime filmmakers, the Living Room Theater (341 SW 10th Avenue; 971–222–2010) combines food and drink service at your seat up to show time, plush recliners, private tables, European style café and lounge— and a large array of independent films. Very importantly, in addition, Portland's Living Room Theater is the first all-digital, only-digital theater in the country.

It should be mentioned that Portland is the destination city for a tremendous percentage of indie films that might open in just a handful of other locations. When money is scarce, distributors will often decide to shell out just for a few target markets. Typically those markets will sound something like Los Angeles, New York, Chicago, San Francisco and, very likely, Portland. For this reason, you can even count on the corporate chain theater of The Fox Tower Stadium 10 (846 SW Park Avenue; 800–326–3264), which is simply devoted to art house and foreign fare. And versus those theaters that jump on the bandwagon after awards' season has proclaimed the nominees and winners, you can nearly set your Academy Award watch by Fox Tower ahead of time. If it plays at Fox Tower, it's got a good chance to be courted by Oscar.

9:30 PM

JAZZ THINGS UP

For the finest, high-end jazz club in Portland, not to mention absolutely delicious Mediterranean fare, head to Jimmy Mak's (221 NW 10th Avenue; 503–295–6542) for dinner, drinks, and a simply wonderful evening of music, including even a Grammy winner in the mix now and then. *USA Today* says, "Don't miss nationally known Jimmy Mak's jazz club," and *Down Beat Magazine* claims that Jimmy Mak's is "one of the world's top 100 places to hear jazz."

The vibe is cool and atmospheric without being at all pompous, and entrees like the feta, herb, and sundried tomato stuffed chicken breast as well as spanokopita, pasticcio, and many other Greek and Middle Eastern favorites round out a perfect evening. Dinner stops at 10:00, but the bar menu continues until closing at 2:00. Music starts at 8:00 nightly, continues until approximately midnight, and reservations are always recommended.

OR...

...if you happen to arrive in town a little too tired and hungry to jump right into cultural events and late night dining, another option could be first to enjoy the exemplary cuisine of one of Portland's premiere celebrity chefs, winner of the 2005 James Beard Foundation's award for Best Chef in the Pacific Northwest, Vitaly Paley, at his own Paley's Place (1204 NW 21st Avenue; 503–243–2403). Starters there consist of such items as citrus cured local salmon with Russian salad and caviar crème fraiche, and entrées smack of crispy sweetbreads en vol-au-vent, local crayfish, morel mushrooms, and asparagus.

Following your meal, then treat yourself to a film event that few screens in the world offer like Portland's.

12:00 AM

SMALL SCREEN

If you still have a little energy left over, and you find yourself psyched for more celluloid, then cozy up in your room with a movie from the hotel's selection of over 400 titles.

SATURDAY

9:00 AM

BON APPETIT

The forecast today calls for a fair share of strides, so no need to go far for brunch. Right there in your hotel, the esteemed Heathman Restaurant serves Saturday brunch from 9:00 to 2:00. Enjoy an Oregon Dungeness crab omelet, a Benedict with pork loin or smoked salmon, or a malted Belgian waffle with a cup of Fonte' coffee from Seattle or a glass of champagne.

10:30 AM

THE PEARL IS YOUR OYSTER

One of the most explosively successful examples of urban renaissance in the entire country, Portland's Pearl District is the art hub of the city with over twenty galleries and art schools. Located in what was once an industrial warehouse area of the city, the Pearl has undergone a complete gentrification makeover and, in addition to being the largest art district in Portland, is home to dozens of high-end shops, bars, clubs, restaurants, and pricey condos. Visit www.explorethepearl.com for a complete list of local establishments as well as a walking map, and make the most of this opportunity to tour a truly fine art district.

12:30 PM

CHINESE OASIS

Sitting like a fortressed mirage in the middle of Portland's Old Town/Chinatown bustle is a city block-sized glimpse into the culture and nature of China. The Portland Classical Chinese Garden (239 NW Everett; 503–228–8131) is operated by a non-profit organization that attempts to explain Chinese customs and traditions as revealed through their millennia of interaction with plants. Consequently, a simple stroll will find you amongst 1000 year-old Camellias nurtured by monks in Portland's sister city of Suzhou, China as well as hundreds of native Chinese plant species and forms, many rare shrubs and perennials, and signature collections of Magnolia, Cymbidium, Osmanthus, Rhododendron, and bamboo.

Enjoy an education in Chinese ethos as you meander meditatively through garden areas with names like "Reflections in Clear Ripples," "Moon Locking Pavilion," and "Celestial Hall of Permeating Fragrance." Guided tours are available daily at noon and 1:00, or you can just let the garden itself guide you through. At some point in your visit, you may also elect to sip a cup of tea poured by Portland's own Tao of Tea in the Tower of Cosmic Reflections, the "most authentic Chinese teahouse in the United States."

2:30 PM

STIFF UPPER LIP

In case you didn't get to take a load off long enough at the Chinese teahouse and/or you're looking for a concoction a little stiffer than steeped leaves, head to the Vault Martini Bar (226 NW 12th Avenue; 503–224–4909) where you can pucker up to a habañero pineapple martini at one of their outdoor tables and sync up to the vibe of one of Portland's most hip and trendy spots.

You have a big dinner coming up in a bit, but if you find yourself in need of a light snack to keep those feet firing, share the Spaniard pizza with quince paste, Serrano, chevre, and manchego or perhaps a s'more fondue.

4:00 PM

CURL UP WITH A GOOD BOOK

Or thousands upon thousands in Portland's promised land

for the devout bookworm! A cultured, highbrow exploration of Portland would be unthinkable without a trip to Powell's City of Books (1005 W. Burnside; 800–878–7323). It may not look like much from the outside, but books shouldn't be judged by their covers, and neither should their stores.

Powell's is a full city block of new and used books divided into sixty distinct sections between nine color coded rooms on four floors. And yes, they provide you with a map.

It is very hard not to get snared by any one of the fabulous rooms and all they offer, therefore plan to spend some time. It is doubtful you've ever been surrounded by this many literary treasures in a commercial setting, so this hunt should be savored.

5:30 PM

DON'T LIFT A FINGER

Not even to pick up the menu or, often harder still, make a decision. At Park Kitchen (422 NW 8th Avenue; 503–223–PARK) chef Scott Dolich and his staff will carefully select for you four fabulous courses from their menu, including dessert, for $45.00 per mouth. With items on their regular menu like pulled pork and sweet pea ravioli and carpaccio of halibut, zucchini, and basil, it's not hard to find a level of trust to take on the chef's tasting menu offered here. Plus, the staff is used to working with vegetarian options and food allergy issues if you have a food sensitivity need.

It should be noted that this special dinner requires two full hours to enjoy, and the restaurant requires that your entire table orders the chef's tasting menu or none at all. As the tasting menu is derived from the regular menu which, as mentioned, is outstanding on its own, if your table elects not to go the tasting menu route, a truly fine dining experience nonetheless awaits you.

8:00 PM

CURTAIN CALL

It's Saturday night, and in Portland all the world's a stage. Unique and fabulous venues, many of them housing more than one theatre, dance, ballet, and opera company, are within walking distance from your hotel. The following is a breakdown of some of the theatres, their size and history, in-house companies, and contact information so that you may paint the town from a palette well defined.

Portland Center for the Performing Arts (main number 503–248–4335) is nationally recognized as one of the top ten performing art centers in the country. PCPA is comprised of five different venues in three separate structures—all in downtown—offering over 900 performances annually ranging from plays and concerts to ballet, lectures, stand-up, Broadway shows, and more.

Originally built in 1917 as the Civic Auditorium, the Keller Auditorium (222 SW Clay) is the largest of the PCPA venues with a seating capacity of 2,992. With two balconies and a very large stage, this is a save-the-ticket-stub kind of theater, regardless of show. In-house companies include Portland Opera, the Oregon Ballet Theatre, and the Oregon Children's Theatre.

Take a few minutes prior to the show to mosey across the street from Keller Auditorium where you'll glimpse one of Portland's playful pastimes. Keller Fountain is an enormous series of flowing pools from which the authorities kindly avert their eyes while the city swims. The fountain is so popular during the summer that, if Pioneer Courthouse Square is considered Portland's living room, then Keller Fountain is its bathtub.

Overlooking Keller Fountain, the Keller Café (503–432–2908) on the second floor of the Auditorium offers dinner, drinks, and dessert before the show. In case you decide to go this route for dinner instead, reservations are strongly recommended.

The second oldest venue of Portland Center for the Performing Arts is also the second largest. Built in 1928, the Arlene Schnitzer Concert Hall (1037 SW Broadway) is a stunning, opulent affair with 2,776 seats, an orchestra pit, and a choir loft. Its iconic "Portland" sign out front heralds a theater that is home to the Oregon Symphony, White Bird Dance Company, Portland Arts and Lectures, and a host of others.

Located inside the spectacular New Theatre Building (1111 SW Broadway) are three different venues: the Newmark Theatre with 880 seats, the Dolores Winningstad Theatre with 292 seats, and Brunish Hall at 200 seats. With all this under one roof, one would think that there would be noise crossover or at the very least patron congestion issues. Such is not the case. This place is a well-oiled, high-end, theatre-going machine, and audience members are completely oblivious to any other theatre than the one they are attending.

The spacious lobby of the New Theatre Building features a five-story rotunda above which is an art-glass "Spectral Light Dome" skylight. Overlooking the lobby are three levels of balconies that are designed like box seats. If you've allowed yourself enough time between dinner and the show, grab a martini from the theatre's own ArtBar & Bistro (503–432–2905) and relax in one of these box seats while people watching theatergoers in the lobby below.

Formally part of the Portland Center for the Performing Arts before branching off on its own and moving into the Gerding Theater, Portland Center Stage (128 NW 11th Avenue; 503–445–3700) is one of the 25 largest theater companies in the United States. Housed inside the historic Armory building dating back to 1891, the company is not located in Portland's Cultural District but, rather, in the nearby Pearl District where you just reveled in your dinner experience.

Well established in the Portland arts' scene and nationally recognized, Artists Repertory Theatre (1515 SW Morrison; 503–241–1278) is a not-for-profit theatre company that stages its productions in two different venues. The main stage is located at the above Morrison address, again not far from your hotel, and the second is in north Portland at the Interstate Firehouse Cultural Center (5340 N Interstate Avenue; 503–823–4322).

Across the Willamette but relatively close, you'll find Theater! Theatre! (3430 SE Belmont). Located in Portland's eclectic and lively Belmont District, which itself is worth the short jaunt, Theater! Theatre! is home to two distinct theatres or stages as well as three different theatre companies.

The first of these venues is Theatre Noir, at 95 seats, which is host year round to Profile Theatre (503–242–0080), one of only two theatre companies in the entire country that showcases one playwright per season.

Next, the Arena Stage at Theater! Theatre! is shared during the year between two companies. Theatre Vertigo (503–306–0870) is a not-for-profit ensemble of theatre artists, and Integrity Productions (503–286–3456) emphasizes the feminine perspective.

10:30 PM

THE SHOW MUST GO ON

And that it will as you and your friend(s) discuss the fine theatre experience you just shared while relaxing around a table in the bistro of Higgins Restaurant and Bar (1239 SW Broadway; 503–222–9070). Greg Higgins is yet one more in Portland's impressive lineup of celebrity chefs, and even his bistro menu this late at night reflects just that.

Appropriately stationed right around the corner from several of the theatre destinations you had to choose from, Higgins offers such treats as a house-made charcuterie plate with their own pickles or a chocolate pumpkin mousse tart or several choices in between. A full bar is on tap as well if you'd like just to sip an after theatre cognac and munch on a plate of honey and chili roasted Oregon hazelnuts while engaging in requisite post-performance banter.

SUNDAY

9:00 AM

SUPPER CLUB BRUNCH

It's not a conundrum. It's brunch. Supper clubs are simply a wonderful new way to reclaim the tradition of communal bread breaking, and they're taking hold in America's finest cuisine capitals, of which we just happen to be one. In the Buckman neighborhood, Simpatica Dining Hall (828 SE Ash; 503–235–1600) is the premiere supper club that hosts dinners every Friday and Saturday night where, by reservation only, everyone is seated at the same time, eats the same meal from a menu pre-set by the chef, and all you have to do is pass the cream sauce. On Sunday morning, however, you'll probably have a table to yourself if you prefer, and you can make the choice between the breakfast fare available.

It should be mentioned that, in addition to being a dining hall and supper club, Simpatica is also a food resource. It has its own charcuterie and butcher shop, Viande Meats, which was recently highlighted by The Food Network, and is where the meats of the dining hall, including those for breakfast, are crafted, cured, smoked, and prepared.

11:00 AM

A PARK RUNS THROUGH IT

As deep as we delve into metaphor and poetry, as high as we reach for symbolic and elevated value, we find that nowhere is the meaning we strive for better articulated than in nature. And nowhere in the city is that fact more succinctly celebrated than in the park that runs for six city blocks and binds together the strands of the Cultural District. Connected to another six blocks of continuous park that shapes the campus of Portland State University, the land for the South Park Blocks, as this enormous park is called, was donated to Portland by a tanner named Daniel Lownsdale in 1849, two years before Portland was an incorporated city. The strip of land remained relatively bare until a City Council authorization in 1877 saw the planting of 104 poplar and elm trees. In 2008, this remains a cherished stand of stately beauty for which generations have been grateful to those members who voted for the shade they knew they'd never experience.

On the west side of the trees, you'll find one of the largest collections of 20th-century art in the Northwest at the Portland Art Museum (1219 SW Park Avenue; 503–226–2811). The collection further includes Asian, European, and Native American art in addition to large traveling exhibits and an outdoor sculpture garden with works by Barbara Hepworth and Pierre Auguste Renoir.

Across the park from the art museum is the Oregon Historical Society (1200 SW Park Avenue; 503–222–1741), which chronicles our state's history from exploration to modern times. Permanent installations include the

Battleship Oregon exhibit and the award winning "Oregon My Oregon" display that tries to explain the state's present by tracing its past.

Originally a hotel built in 1923, the building that houses the Historical Society boasts an eight-story mural depicting the Lewis and Clark expedition that has a must-see optical illusionary effect of being three dimensional.

The grand architecture and unique sound of the historic churches of the Cultural District should likewise not be missed. Without exception the following churches are regular hosts to guest performers, authors, and lecturers and/or offer concerts of their own to the public. Concerts and recitals by professional musicians from around the globe are common in these churches and may provide a stimulating option for your afternoon as you continue to explore the Cultural District.

The First Congregational United Church of Christ (1126 SW Park Avenue; 503–228–7219) was built in 1891 in the Venetian Gothic style, and its organ, comprised of 3,100 pipes, dates back to 1871.

The St. James Lutheran Church (1315 SW Park Avenue; 503–227–2439) was built in 1890 and has a Gothic Revival edifice. And similar to the other churches listed here, St. James Lutheran features the beautiful stained glass windows created by the famous Povey Brothers Art Glass Works, which ran its unique business in Portland from 1888 to 1929. (Further examples of Povey glass can be found at the Pittock Mansion, Huber's Restaurant, and several homes in the Irvington District.)

Two blocks from the South Park Blocks but worth the short stroll is The Old Church (1422 SW 11th Avenue; 503–222–2031). Built in 1882 and designed by the architect Warren H. William, who is largely responsible for the abundance of Victorian architecture in Portland, The Old Church's location was originally criticized for being "too far out in the country." Smack dab in the middle of what is now downtown, the quaint old dame of a church is the only local host to a Hook and Hastings pipe organ, which is also the oldest tracker-organ in the Northwest still in its original location, dating back to 1883. (A tracker-organ uses mechanical connections instead of electricity to produce its sound, and it was fashionable for a time to convert these instruments to electricity. The Old Church's pipe organ never was, however, thus preserving its valued and rare status.)

Also on the South Park Blocks, at the northern border of Portland State University, sits the school's oldest building, Lincoln Hall (1620 SW Park Avenue; main PSU number 503–725–3000). Built in 1911 in the Classical Revival style complete with Corinthian columns at its entry, Lincoln Hall is the center of the campus' performing arts. It houses three separate venues and a nearly continuous roster of new and changing performances and events, many of them free of charge.

2:00 PM

SO MANY CHOICES

You've been exploring the Cultural District for a while, and now is the time to decide whether you will continue the tour or pick from one of the many venues and enjoy a Sunday matinee. Many of the churches as well as Lincoln Hall listed just above in addition to the theatres broken down under Saturday's event options will offer a Sunday show of esteemed proportions. The options should be varied and plentiful, and most of them will be at your toe-tips. Only you know your remaining energy level, but the city's performing arts are here for you if you wish to partake. Otherwise, continue your walking investigation of the Cultural District. You haven't even made a dent.

4:30 PM

THE PERFECT TICKET

Also situated on the South Park Blocks as its name implies, Southpark (901 SW Salmon; 503–326–1300) has woven itself firmly into the Portland Cultural District. It offers a sophisticated wine scene, complete with its own Wine Director, and goes to the trouble to conjure up homemade ginger infused vodka and cucumber infused gin. For a light bite, you may order something like the salmon cakes or veggie crepe in the bar, or, for something more hearty, dishes like the duck confit with risotto and dried cherries or the bacon wrapped prawn stuffed trout will likely be worth an ovation—undoubtedly inspiring you to compose a Portland encore.

Important Side Note: From essentially Cinco de Mayo through Oktoberfest, the Portland area plays host to a tremendous array of outdoor festivals, concerts, plays, and parades. The ultimate Portland party is, of course, The Rose Festival (503–227–2681), a century-old tradition that goes on for weeks and peaks on the first and second weekends in June. In addition to the festivals, including cool ones devoted to beer and wine (503–778–5917; 503–595–0891), Portland absolutely buzzes during the summer months with everything from Shakespeare-in-the-park to outdoor concerts at Tom McCall Waterfront Park, Washington Park, and more (503–467–6573; 503–823–PLAY). So check out the websites at the end of this chapter, research ahead and see if your scheduled trip coincides with any of these events and be flexible to include at least one if you desire to add further local flavor to your respite.

Also, if you're willing to extend the boundaries of your visit beyond Portland, not enough can possibly be said about the Oregon Shakespeare Festival (800–219–8161). Located in Ashland, in the southwestern part of the state, the Oregon Shakespeare Festival is an eight-and-a-half-month long homage to all things theatre. People from around the world flock to this small hamlet of 20,000 people that is transformed into a metropolitan, bustling theatre mecca during the festival. Every year Ashland's curtain opens on eleven different plays, some Shakespeare, some more modern, on three different stages for a total of more than 770 performances, drawing approximately 360,000 people. This is nothing less than a theatergoer's dream playbill.

65

The Skinny

Lay Your Head

The Heathman Hotel 1001 SW Broadway at Salmon;
800–551–0011; www.heathmanhotel.com

Cool Your Heels

ArtBar & Bistro 1111 SW Broadway; 503–432–2905;
www.pcpa.com
Higgins Restaurant and Bar 1239 SW Broadway; 503–
222–9070; www.higgins.citysearch.vista.com
Jimmy Mak's 221 NW 10th Avenue; 503–295–6542;
www.jimmymaks.com
Keller Café 222 SW Clay; 503–432–2908; www.pcpa.com
Paley's Place 1204 NW 21st Avenue; 503–243–2403;
www.paleysplace.net
Park Kitchen 422 NW 8th Avenue; 503–223–PARK;
www.parkkitchen.com
Simpatica Dining Hall 828 SE Ash; 503–235–1600;
www.simpaticacatering.com
Southpark 901 SW Salmon; 503–326–1300;
www.southparkseafood.com

Tao of Tea 239 NW Everett; 503–224–8455;
www.taooftea.com
Vault Martini 226 NW 12th Avenue; 503–224–4909;
www.vault–martini.com

Actions Speak Louder Than Words

Arlene Schnitzer Concert Hall 1037 SW Broadway; 503–
248–4335; www.pcpa.com
Artists Repertory Theatre 1515 SW Morrison; 503–241–
1278; www.artistsrep.org
Brunish Hall 1111 SW Broadway; 503–248–4335;
www.pcpa.com
Cinema 21 616 NW 21st Avenue; 503–223–4515;
www.cinema21.com
Clinton Street Theater 2522 SE Clinton; 503–238–8899;
www.clintonsttheater.com
Concerts-in-the-Parks 503–823–PLAY;
www.portlandonline.com/parks/
Dolores Winningstad Theatre 1111 SW Broadway; 503–
248–4335; www.pcpa.com
First Congregational United Church of Christ 1126 SW
Park Avenue; 503–228–7219; www.uccportland.org
Fox Tower Stadium 10 846 SW Park Avenue; 800–326–
3264; www.regalcinemas.com
Hollywood Theatre 4122 NE Sandy; 503–281–4215;
www.hollywoodtheatre.org
Indie Wine Festival 503–595–0891;
www.indiewinefestival.com
Integrity Productions 3430 SE Belmont; 503–286–3456;
www.integrityproductions.org
Interstate Firehouse Cultural Center 5340 N Interstate
Avenue; 503–823–4322; www.ifcc–arts.org

Keller Auditorium 222 SW Clay; 503–248–4335; www.pcpa.com

Lincoln Hall 1620 SW Park Avenue; main PSU number 503–725–3000; www.pdx.edu/events/1606/

Living Room Theater 341 SW 10th Avenue; 971–222–2010; www.livingroomtheaters.com

Newmark Theatre 1111 SW Broadway; 503–248–4335; www.pcpa.com

New Theatre Building 1111 SW Broadway; 503–248–4335; www.pcpa.com

Northwest Film Center 1219 SW Park Avenue; 503–221–1156; www.nwfilm.org

The Old Church 1422 SW 11th Avenue; 503–222–2031; www.oldchurch.org

Oregon Brewers Festival 503–778–5917; www.oregonbrewfest.com

Oregon Historical Society 1200 SW Park Avenue; 503–222–1741; www.ohs.org

Oregon Shakespeare Festival 800–219–8161; www.osfashland.org

Portland Art Museum 1219 SW Park Avenue; 503–226–2811; www.portlandartmuseum.org

Portland Center for the Performing Arts main number 503–248–4335; www.pcpa.com

Portland Center Stage 128 NW 11th Avenue; 503–445–3700; www.pcs.org

Portland Classical Chinese Garden 239 NW Everett; 503–228–8131; www.portlandchinesegarden.org

Profile Theatre 3430 SE Belmont; 503–242–0080; www.profiletheatre.org

Rose Festival 503–227–2681; www.rosefestival.org

Shakespeare-in-the-Parks 503–467–6573; www.portlandactors.com

St. James Lutheran Church 1315 SW Park Avenue; 503–

227–2439; www.stjameslutheranportland.org
Theater! Theatre! 3430 SE Belmont;
www.integrityproductions.org; www.profiletheatre.org;
www.theatrevertigo.org
Theatre Vertigo 3430 SE Belmont; 503–306–0870;
www.theatrevertigo.org

Get It In Gear

Powell's City of Books 1005 W. Burnside; 800–878–7323;
www.powells.com

Check Under the 'Hood

Belmont
www.portlandneighborhood.com/belmont.html

Buckman
www.portlandneighborhood.com/buckman.html

Downtown
www.portlandneighborhood.com/downtown–portland.html

Nob Hill
www.portlandneighborhood.com/nobhill.html

Old Town / Chinatown
http://www.portlandneighborhood.com/oldtown.html

Pearl District
www.portlandneighborhood.com/pearldistrict.html

Richmond
www.portlandneighborhood.com/richmond.html

Cheap Weekend

Avalon, Belmont St.

P ortlander's slang word for expensive is "spendy," as in *"I'd love to buy that sweater, but it's kind of spendy."* If you look up *spendy* in a standard dictionary, you probably won't find it. That being the case, it is an urban slang word that means something of a cross between expensive and trendy. Sometimes locals refer to the trendy shopping district along NW 23rd Avenue as "SpendyThird."

Of course you don't have to have a spendy weekend in Portland to have a great time. The focus of this chapter then is on experiencing the unique and wonderful weirdness that is Portland, on a reasonable budget.

FRIDAY

6:00 PM

HOSTEL ACTION

If you're visiting Portland, hostels provide an inexpensive lodging option for travelers who are willing to share some common living space with fellow explorers on a budget. Some hostels offer co-ed dorms and even private rooms. The following are two local hostels run by Hostelling International, located in the popular Portland neighborhoods of Hawthorne and Nob Hill.

Hostelling International is a member-based organization. Memberships may be purchased upon arrival and are good for one year at any H.I. hostel the world over. The annual membership cost is $28 for an adult, $18 for those over 55, and youths under 18 get one free. Or you can get a temporary membership for $3 per night. In addition to the membership fee, you'll pay for your room reservation, which will run approximately $17 for a dorm room to $48 for a private room (prices may vary depending on season).

Side Note: Being a traveler's hostel, people who live in Portland and the surrounding area are not able to stay here. Consider staying at our suggested HOTEL OPTION instead.

Hostelling International–Portland Hawthorne Hostel (3031 SE Hawthorne; 503–236–3380) is located in the Hawthorne District in SE Portland. This hostel features a fully equipped kitchen that you may use during your stay and is conveniently located within walking distance to a grocery store, shopping, cafes, and more in one of Portland's most popular urban neighborhoods.

Hostelling International–Northwest Portland International Hostel & Guesthouse (425 NW 18th Avenue (& Glisan Street); 503–241–2783) can be found in the popular Northwest area known as Nob Hill, a neighborhood full of shopping and dining options. Staying here, you will be very centrally located. Only blocks from Downtown and the popular Pearl District, this hostel setting affords you the opportunity to walk conveniently or take public transportation to many great destinations.

HOTEL OPTION

Of course, if a hostel is not your cup of tea, you'll want an inexpensive hotel option. And since you're in Portland, you won't want to stay any place boring or run-of-the-mill. Located in North Portland's Industrial area near the waterfront, in the Eliot neighborhood, McMenamin's White Eagle Rock 'n' Roll Hotel (836 N Russell; 866–271–3377) offers the added benefit of being situated only a block from the TriMet MAX Light Rail station (yellow line), making public transportation easy and certainly more affordable than renting a car.

The White Eagle isn't a fancy hotel, but it is affordably priced for a small hotel that is anything but ordinary. Nightly rates range from about $30–$60 for a simple room furnished with antiques. And, while affordably priced, this isn't the Motel 6. Reputedly haunted by spirits from the dark days of Portland's brothels and Shanghai tunnels, this historic brick hotel opened in 1905 and still oozes yesteryear's rustic, somewhat Old West charm. Located just above the White Eagle Saloon, nightly rock and roll might keep you awake, but the free entertainment and lively atmosphere will make for a memorable, if not restful, weekend.

7:00 PM

WINGIN' IT PORTLAND STYLE

Nothing beats a sloppy mess of BBQ chicken wings for a tasty dinner that won't cost an arm and a leg. Luckily, only a short trip away from your hotel is one of North Portland's finest original wing joints. Fire on the Mountain (4225 N Interstate Avenue; 503–280–WINGS) serves real Buffalo-style chicken wings with your choice of homemade sauce made daily from scratch. In addition to a couple sauce options that rotate each month, you can choose to smother your wings (and face) in the following taste bonanza: Mild, Medium, Hot, Extra Hot, El Jefé, Sweet BBQ, Jamaican Jerk, "Soon to be Famous" Spicy Peanut, Raspberry Habañero, and Tequila Chipotle.

Of course the wings don't fly solo. They ride with the usual sidekicks of celery sticks with blue cheese or ranch dressing and several delicious side options like fries and onion rings. Fire on the Mountain also offers a few vegetarian menu options such as the meatless "Portland Wings" as well as menu choices for the kiddies. And let's face it—this is probably not the healthiest meal you're going to eat. So, if you're going for the gusto you might as well throw caution to the wind and have some dessert. Might we suggest a heart stopping fried Twinkie topped with powdered sugar? No kidding. It's so very bad, and yet oh so good. A stack of nine chicken wings and a mountain of french fries will set you back about $9.

Tip: If you're feeling amazingly gluttonous or lazy and would rather eat your wings n' Twinkie feast right in your hotel room, then try the Portland restaurant delivery service known as Delivered Dish (503–239–0100). For a nominal delivery fee, they will deliver food to your home or hotel directly from Fire on the Mountain as well as from several other Portland restaurants. Just go to their website listed at the end of this chapter, select your food choices from the restaurant menus, submit your payment information and then sit back and wait for your food to arrive.

OR...

...WHEN IN PORTLAND, DO AS...

Knowing you want to eat on a reasonable budget but also knowing you want to experience the uniqueness of Portland and not just eat at a fast food joint you can find in Any-town, USA, we think a visit to one of Portland's favorite restaurants for late night dining is in order. Le Bistro Mon-tage (301 SE Morrison; 503–234–1324) is so popular it has its own urban slang. Locals simply call it "The Montage." *"Specializing in fine dining for the low-rent and late-night crowds,"* Montage's menu has a range of offerings from good old macaroni and cheese (with several variations to choose from) to jambalaya and alligator bites.

You'll want to come to the Montage with a spirit of "When in Rome, do as the Roman's Do," because this isn't a private dining environment where you can quietly fade into the background and observe the local culture. Instead, you'll enjoy the convivial atmosphere while seated at communal tables, dining side-by-side with fellow visitors and other Portlanders. The quirkiness of the establishment even continues after you've gone home since all leftovers are creatively wrapped up in extravagant and fanciful tin-foil sculptures. Average price range for dinner is about $10-$20.

9:30 PM

DANCING FEET

If you're in a dancing mood, Holocene (1001 SE Morrison;

503–239–7639) is a popular Portland destination catering to the stylish club set. Not far from Le Bistro Montage and likewise located in the Buckman neighborhood, Holocene features local musicians and DJs and has modern décor, a nice sized dance floor, and several separate spaces including an indoor area for smokers. The cover charge ranges from free to a few bucks. Visit their website to view the events' calendar, so you'll know what to expect before you go.

SATURDAY

8:00 AM

M–M–M–M, GRAVY

Ok, so Gravy (3957 N Mississippi; 503–287–8800) isn't the cheapest restaurant for breakfast in Portland, but it is one of the best. Plus, the meal portions at Gravy are so enormous that you can easily split your meal with two or even three people if you so choose. This restaurant is extremely popular on weekends, so get there early to avoid a wait. After about 9:00 AM, people are lining up on the sidewalk. If that is the case, put your name in and stroll up to one of the coffee shops on the street, like Fresh Pot (4001 N Mississippi; 503–284–8928), so you can enjoy some coffee while you wait for a table to become available.

Of course, with a name like Gravy, it's no surprise that one of the best choices on the menu is biscuits and gravy, including the vegetarian kind. Also, they're known for their crispy and delicious nest of hash browns, sweet potato pancakes, and fantastic omelets and scrambles.

9:30 AM

THIS SIDE OF THE MISSISSIPPI

After breakfast, take a stroll up and down Mississippi Avenue and enjoy all the distinctive shops and businesses of this unique area, simply one-of-a-kind Portland stores that you won't discover anyplace else. Mississippi Avenue is in the Boise neighborhood, an area that has been heavily affected by gentrification, a topic that is always controversial as memories run deep and resistance runs strong.

On the surface, much of Mississippi remains a mix. Earlier days are reflected in the tone and style of architecture lining the street, but housed within are predominantly businesses that have opened their doors in just the past couple of years. And regardless of gentrification controversy, the new entrepreneurs who are hanging out their shingles and giving their businesses a go in this neighborhood seem to represent quintessential Portland—that is, having the courage to try ones own thing.

And, since the focus of this chapter is about watching the wallet, here are two Portland businesses along Mississippi Avenue that are thrifty standouts:

The ReBuilding Center (3625 N Mississippi Avenue; 503–331–1877) just ain't the Home Depot—true to Portland's green heart. The ReBuilding Center is all about reuse and low impact environmental building as well as reconstruction. The Center is the largest non-profit used building materials' resource in North America. Even if you're visiting from out of town and building supplies sound a little large for the suitcase you brought, it's worth a visit if you enjoy historical house items and thrift shopping, or if you're an artist, craftsman, environmentalist, or just plain curious. Featuring genuine old house parts with an inventory that is in a constant state of flux, you might find hardware, windows, doors … and even the original kitchen sink. Simply, this is a fun place to explore and find inspiration.

The Black Rose Collective (4038 N Mississippi Avenue) markets themselves as *"A community owned business based on the principles of cooperation, not competition. Serving the rich cultural and economic diversity of our neighborhood."* Black Rose features new and used books, and in addition they provide neighborhood Freecycling, where neighbors can drop off items for which they no longer have use, but others might.

"Changing the world one gift at a time." Portland Freecycling is a grassroots movement of people who are giving and receiving free items to encourage re-use and lower our impact on landfills and the planet. Members can post their goods on this list as long as the item is free, appropriate for all ages, and legal. Cost to join—free!

12:00 PM

LEONARDO DA BARISTA

If it's time to recharge your batteries with a nice caffeinated beverage, head north on Mississippi Avenue and visit The Albina Press (4637 North Albina; 503–282–5214). All of the espresso drinks are divine and made with an artisan's attention to brewing the perfect cup every single time. The blend of flavors in your cup are luscious, complex, and unexpected if you are unknowingly accustomed to drinking a lesser quality brew. Your latte or hot chocolate will be a work of art and in fact will most likely boast a work of art etched into the crema on top.

Continuing the theme, Albina Press is also a local art gallery, the walls showcasing a rotating selection of artwork for your enjoyment. So relax in the pleasant atmosphere, grab a local newspaper, plug in your laptop (free Wi-Fi) or just sit in the window and observe a moment in the life of Portland.

1:00 PM

WHY NOT LUNCH?

Try lunch at one of Portland's best little taquerias, ¿Por Qué No? (3524 N Mississippi; 503–467–4149). Teeny tiny on the inside, the restaurant will have you feeling certain victory if you end up snatching one of the last tables available. If the weather cooperates, you may opt for a patio table outside and take it easy.

¿Por Qué No? uses quality meat and local produce and is famous for its fresh and delicious guacamole. Of course, the tortillas are made fresh by hand, and the service is casual and friendly.

But if you'd like to sample a few nationalities in addition to Mexican, another reasonable and tasty option just down the street is Laughing Planet (3765 N Mississippi; 503–467–4146). They feature big burritos and quesadillas in addition to dishes like rice bowls and salads, and a filling meal will only set you back about $5-$6 or so for lunch. Featuring hormone free chicken and organic tofu or tempeh, you can dine really well on a budget and feel good about what you're eating.

2:30 PM

PORTLAND'S CRAFTY SIDE

The Portland Saturday Market (503–222–6072) is our infamous local arts and crafts' market that is a "don't miss" stop on any visit. Located in Old Town/Chinatown under the Burnside Bridge at SW Naito Parkway and SW 1st Avenue, the open-air market is bustling every Saturday and Sunday from March through Christmas Eve. Always a fun place simply to browse (and people watch), you'll find some unique gifts in every price range.

With everything from pottery, jewelry, and artwork to home accessories and pet products, you're sure to find something to please someone. Plus you'll be supporting a thriving Portland-based arts and crafts' institution that's been around since 1974. The market also features live musical entertainment and performance artists. And if you're hungry, enjoy a bite from the Saturday Market food court.

5:00 PM

RELAX, RENEW, REFRESH

Now it's time to unplug the brain, let go and unwind before dinner. And since you're probably used to the notion that the words, "massage" and "budget" aren't typically paired, then you might just enjoy letting a licensed massage therapist at East West College (525 NE Oregon; 503–233–6500) rub that idea right out of your head. The East West College Professional Clinic is open to the public on Saturday with appointment times from 9:00 AM to 7:00 PM. Prices are $45 for a 60-minute massage—almost half of what you might pay for the same treatment at a more spendy spa. If you want to splurge, it's $65 for a 90-minute massage. Remember to call ahead to make your appointment, so the massage will fit into your itinerary.

6:30 PM

PHOENICIAN JOURNEY

We're pretty sure just about every Portland local has eaten at Nicholas Restaurant (318 SE Grand; 503–235–5123) or at least heard about how good it is. Nicholas started as a true Mom and Pop restaurant founded in 1986 and has since become a local legend. As they say, *"The link between ancient Phoenicia and Lebanon today is manifested in the continuity of culinary traditions that place food at the centre of social and ritual life."* Clearly much love and attention is given to maintaining the history of family recipes passed down through generations.

Nicholas features delicious homemade Middle Eastern fare with huge portions that can easily feed two people and meal prices ranging from a few bucks to twenty bucks, with most averaging under ten dollars. As with most popular Portland restaurants, this restaurant can fill up quickly, so expect a wait. But a dip in the hummus will help you get over it.

8:00 PM

HAUNTED COFFEE

Portlanders think nothing of drinking coffee at any time of the day or night. And, since your last cup of java has long since worn off, it's time for another jolt of caffeine and some delicious dessert to propel you into your evening. Stop in for a visit at one of our most eccentric and original coffee houses, Rimsky-Korsakoffee (707 SE 12th Avenue; 503–232–2640) and enjoy the peculiar ambiance that has been described as a little bit "Addams Family." Rumor has it that there are a few haunted tables in this coffee house, and to appreciate the full experience of the unusual atmosphere, be sure to visit the bathrooms. This coffee house is cozy, quirky, distinctive, and a lot of fun.

9:00 PM

KAMONIWANNAKARAOKE

Get in touch with your inner Kahuna while singing your heart out at one of Portland's favorite Tiki bars, the Alibi Restaurant and Lounge (4024 N Interstate Avenue; 503–

287–5335). With a big flashy neon sign out front and vintage '50's Polynesian décor inside, it's the closest thing you might find to the big island—or Vegas—in Portland. They serve fried food (with a free food buffet Saturday at midnight) and the requisite Tiki bar fruity drinks with decorative umbrellas.

Unlike Holocene, this isn't a stylish "see and be seen" kind of club. This is all about pure retro kitsch. So check your inhibitions at the puka and catch some tunes as well as the wave.

SUNDAY

8:30 AM

TRIFECTA! ART–BEER–WAFFLES

Welcome to Portland's version of waffle house extraordinaire—Jace Gáce (2045 SE Belmont; 503–239–1887). This isn't a greasy truck stop however; Portland's latest waffle house is actually an art gallery, café, and bar all rolled into one. Art, beer, and waffles might not seem like words that go together when describing a single restaurant, but here in Portland somehow it all works. Jáce Gáce waffles are creative concoctions with menu choices including both sweet and savory.

10:00 AM

BIPED BREAKTHROUGH

By now it should be pretty clear that Portland is full of many diverse neighborhoods, and Southeast Portland offers a couple of the great ones to explore: Belmont and Hawthorne, which are perfect for walking. The slow pace of walking ensures you can see and feel everything up close and personal so you'll really get a sense of the neighborhood. And you can't beat walking for cheap.

So first, let's take a stroll up Belmont Street. With a focus on independently owned Portland shops, the following are just a few notable places of interest you might want to see.

Anthem Records (828 SE 34th Avenue; 503–963–9000) is one of those dying breeds of indie record stores well stocked with not only some of those harder-to-find items but also with helpful and informative employees who are surprisingly unpretentious. You see, whenever we visit a little independent record store, we're reminded of the movie *High Fidelity*. We almost expect some militant record store Nazi to treat us like second-class citizens because of our inferior lack of musical knowledge. Don't worry though, you won't experience any *High Fidelity* flashbacks here—but you'll probably find the soundtrack.

Movie Madness (4320 SE Belmont; 503–234–4363) is likely the most interesting video store you will ever enter. Whatever movie you're looking for, they have it, plus a movie museum. The only way this picture could be any bigger is if DeMille made it. And even then we're not so

86

sure. At 33,000 DVD titles and 27,000 VHS titles, if Movie Madness isn't the largest video store in the world, then it's certainly a contender. Officially recognized by the Southern California Motion Picture Council for its outstanding contribution to the entertainment industry, Movie Madness is to movies what Powell's is to books.

1:00 PM

BOHEMIAN PORTLAND

How could you not enjoy lunch in a place as quirky as the Pied Cow (3244 SE Belmont; 503–230–4866)? Southeast Portland is known for having a bit of a bohemian, hippie flair to it, and, as you take a trip through the Sunnyside neighborhood on the way to southeast Hawthorne, you can easily see how the Pied Cow captures the wonderful spirit of casual, laid-back fun just perfectly. Housed in an old Victorian, Pied Cow offers an amusing menu with a selection of small plates, vegetarian/vegan food, desserts, coffee, tea, beer, wine—and you can even smoke down a hookah outside on the patio as you soak up the Southeast Portland culture.

2:00 PM

BLACK HOLE OF FUN

Portland's go-to source for hours of economical old-school and digital fun is Electric Castle's Wunderland (3451 SE Belmont; 503–238–1617). In addition to their own onsite movie theatre, The Avalon, admission to which is likewise reasonable, Wunderland offers over a hundred different games, all of them operated by nickels. In addition to classic and traditional arcade games, you'll also find air hockey, skee ball, and racing games.

Spend $2.50 for admission, and games are between one and four nickels each. (Even with inflation, these are still retro prices.) All in all, a couple hours of childlike fun will set you back about $5.

3:30 PM

A WORLD OF BEANS AT YOUR TOETIPS

Before you take another step, you're going to need a boost of energy. So, since we're talking cheap, I've got five words for you: "one dollar French pressed coffee!" And better yet, it's Stumptown (3356 SE Belmont; 503–232–8889)! This fantastic Portland coffee shop is renowned locally and even worldwide because of those—you know who you are—who have sampled the goods then smuggled out a few bags of exquisite coffee beans in their suitcase to destinations unknown. (Visit the Annex next door to smuggle some of your own bags home.)

If you haven't had Stumptown coffee, you don't know what you are missing, and, even if you are not a coffee lover, you'll acquire a nasty habit after just one sip. The free Wi–Fi is an added bonus.

4:00 PM

KEEP ON TREKKING

Now we'll take on Hawthorne. Again, there are many wonderful shops to explore, and most are unique to Portland. We've highlighted just a couple.

Presents of Mind (3633 SE Hawthorne; 503–230–7740) is always a fun visit, known for its great selection of hilarious cards, fun t-shirts, gag gifts, baby gifts, jewelry, stationary, and more. If you need to pick up a gift for another or just a mental pick-me-up for yourself, go in and check out cards that will make you smile, and, yes, these are the ones—they'll make you laugh out loud.

What thrifty shopper doesn't want to treasure hunt for bargains at a vintage clothing store? At Red Light Clothing Exchange (3590 SW Hawthorne; 503–963–8888) it's like shopping in your friend's closet, if that closet were the size of a warehouse. You're bound to find something to add to your wardrobe in this cavernous store of new, used, vintage, and consignment items. And, if you're willing to spend some time digging through the bins and clearance merchandise, you might just unearth a real vintage gem.

It should be mentioned that one of the best things about Portland is its abundance of park choices throughout the city. You can literally get away from it all and escape to a serenely beautiful location and yet still be in town. In Southeast Portland at the end of Hawthorne Boulevard, you can even visit a volcano, albeit an extinct one, right within the city. So to complete the perfect trip down Hawthorne, take a stroll to the easily reached peak of Mt. Tabor, named after the Mt. Tabor near Nazareth, for spectacular views of Portland.

Exploring Mt. Tabor Walking Map:
503–823–PLAY

Portland Park's and Recreation—Mt. Tabor Information:
503–823–PLAY

7:00 PM

OPERATION: MOVIE FREEDOM

The Bagdad Theater and Pub (3702 SE Hawthorne; 503–249–7474), with its blazing neon sign and Mediterranean-ish façade, is a popular icon of Hollywood's Golden Age and a recognizable landmark on Hawthorne Boulevard. The Bagdad originally opened in 1927 and has been the site of countless vaudeville shows, movies, and even an Oregon premiere or two, including *One Flew Over a Cuckoo's Nest* in 1975. Now featuring second run (and cheap) movies, this wonderful old movie palace has been entertaining Portlanders for nearly four generations.

Best of all, you can enjoy pizza and a beer as you watch some of the last images of a weekend of lasting images.

The Skinny

Lay Your Head

Hostelling International–Northwest Portland International Hostel & Guesthouse 425 NW 18th Avenue (& Glisan Street); 503–241–2783;
www.2oregonhostels.com/nw_home.htm
Hostelling International–Portland Hawthorne Hostel 3031 SE Hawthorne; 503–236–3380;
www.portlandhostel.org/FAQ.htm
McMenamin's White Eagle Rock 'n' Roll Hotel 836 N Russell; 866–271–3377; www.mcmenamins.com

Cool Your Heels

Albina Press 4637 North Albina; 503–282–5214
Alibi Restaurant and Lounge 4024 N Interstate Avenue; 503–287–5335
Le Bistro Montage 301 SE Morrison; 503–234–1324;
www.montageportland.com
Delivered Dish 503–239–0100; www.delivereddish.com
Fire on the Mountain 4225 N Interstate Avenue; 503–280–WINGS; www.portlandwings.com
Fresh Pot 4001 N Mississippi; 503–284–8928
Gravy 3957 N Mississippi; 503–287–8800

Holocene 1001 SE Morrison; 503–239–7639; www.holocene.org
Jáce Gáce 2045 SE Belmont; 503–239–1887; www.jacegace.com
Laughing Planet 3765 N Mississippi; 503–467–4146; www.laughingplanetcafe.com
Nicholas Restaurant 318 SE Grand; 503–235–5123; www.nicholasrestaurant.com
Pied Cow 3244 SE Belmont; 503–230–4866
¿Por Qué No? 3524 N Mississippi; 503–467–4149
Rimsky-Korsakoffee 707 SE 12th Avenue; 503–232–2640
Stumptown 3356 SE Belmont; 503–232–8889; www.stumptowncoffee.com

Actions Speak Louder Than Words

Bagdad Theater and Pub 3702 SE Hawthorne; 503–249–7474; www.mcmenamins.com
Electric Castle's Wunderland 3451 SE Belmont; 503–238–1617; www.wunderlandgames.com
Mt. Tabor Information 503–823–PLAY; http://www.portlandonline.com/parks/finder/index.cfm?action=ViewPark&PropertyID=275
Mt. Tabor Walking Map 503–823–PLAY; http://www.portlandonline.com/shared/cfm/image.cfm?id=88124
Portland Saturday Market SW Naito Parkway and SW 1st Avenue; 503–222–6072; www.portlandsaturdaymarket.com

Get It In Gear

Anthem Records 828 SE 34th Avenue; 503–963–9000;
www.anthemrecordsinc.com
Black Rose Collective 4038 N Mississippi Avenue;
www.blackrose.revolt.org/index.html
Movie Madness 4320 SE Belmont; 503–234–4363;
www.moviemadnessvideo.com
Portland Freecycle
http://tribes.tribe.net/freecycleportland;
http://groups.yahoo.com/group/freecycleportland
Presents of Mind 3633 SE Hawthorne; 503–230–7740;
www.presentsofmind.tv
ReBuilding Center 3625 N Mississippi Avenue; 503–331–
1877; www.rebuildingcenter.org
Red Light Clothing Exchange 3590 SW Hawthorne; 503–
963–8888

It's All About You

East West College Professional Clinic 525 NE Oregon;
503–233–6500; www.eastwestcollege.com

Check Under the 'Hood

Belmont
www.portlandneighborhood.com/belmont.html

Buckman
www.portlandneighborhood.com/buckman.html

Eliot
www.portlandneighborhood.com/eliot.html

Hawthorne
www.portlandneighborhood.com/hawthorne.html

Mississippi / Boise
www.portlandneighborhood.com/boise–eliot.html

Nob Hill
www.portlandneighborhood.com/nobhill.html

Old Town / Chinatown
www.portlandneighborhood.com/oldtown.html

Sunnyside
www.portlandneighborhood.com/sunnyside.html

Nature Weekend

Nesting Bird, Oaks Bottom Wildlife Refuge

Portland sits at the perfect confluence of a nestled inland location, a mild winter latitude, rich volcanic soil, and two major rivers. Stir to combine, and you have the ideal recipe for a wildlife haven in a lush landscape. Top off this concoction with an umbrella or two to accent the community that sprang up along with the foliage, and you have an active, combined neighborhood where the effort is not only to coexist with our natural heritage but to protect it, celebrate it, ultimately revel in it.

No party's complete without guests. So please enjoy!

FRIDAY

6:00 PM

BABY STEPS

It's early evening, and you just arrived to town, so we'll introduce you to the new environment with a casual nature walk to begin your stay. Located in north Portland's St. Johns neighborhood, near the junction of the Columbia and Willamette Rivers, is the Smith and Bybee Lakes Wildlife Area. Comprised of 2000 acres, it forms one of the nation's largest urban freshwater wetlands. While there you may enjoy a casual hike of less than a mile along the paved Inter-lakes Trail, which passes through the area's riparian forest habitat and has two wildlife viewing platforms, one on Smith Lake and one on Bybee.

You should know that where the trail begins is not at all clearly marked. When you first enter the park from N. Marine Drive there is a pullover where the ground is marked, "Bus Only," and they mean it. But right there is a tiny post with a microscopic sign that reads, "40-Mile Loop." This is obviously where the 40-Mile Loop (explained more fully in the Active Weekend chapter) continues on the northern edge of Portland. Park your car further down on the left in the small lot. Then return to this sign. As you face the sign, make a right and continue westerly down the path for twenty paces or less. At that point, another path will veer off to your left, leaving the 40-Mile Loop. Take that path to your left, and in another twenty paces or so a much-welcomed sign will guide you the rest of the way.

Side note: A sign as you enter the park warns that the gates will be locked at dusk. One man's dusk is another man's bluehour, but according to harbor security the gates are locked sometime between 9:30 and 10:00 year round, so you have plenty of time to enjoy the park without worrying about having to pitch a tent.

8:00 PM

CAMP PAMPER

You can sleep with the bugs anywhere, but this weekend is to be treated like a vacation. Plus we want to show you around the city. So, during the day you may go toe-to-toe with your inner ranger, but at night you'll be able to eat from real dishes and shower without quarters and strangers. Besides, the objective of most fine hotels appears to be to cushion their guests from the outside world, to create an atmosphere of haven from harshness or at the very least respite from anything beyond the hotel doors. However, some hotels understand that the outside world surrounding them is actually sublime, and they want you to bathe in it. Such is the case with RiverPlace Hotel (1510 SW Harbor Way; 800–227–1333) where river life, ambience, and activities absolutely await your immersion. Staying here, you will have easy access to both an active wildlife experience *and* downtown city life. Then, when relaxation is in order, you may wile away the hours on one of the hotel veranda's rocking chairs overlooking the river and all there to enjoy it.

Side note: If camping is a priority for you, Oregon certainly has no shortage of options. Check out the camping websites listed at the end of this chapter for campground ideas in the Portland area, on the coast, along the Columbia Gorge, as well as throughout Oregon.

9:00 PM

STONE'S THROW

Located right in your hotel is where even the locals go for destination dining. Three Degrees offers northwestern fare like King Salmon as well as striking views of the Willamette River. If your visit coincides with the peak of summer, ask for a seat on the terrace. (This is yet another benefit of Portland's latitude. At 9:00 on a summer's eve, it won't be dark outside when you take your table, and you will be able to enjoy the colors of dusk as they settle in for the night across the water.)

10:30 PM

RIVERBANK STROLL

You have a busy day planned for tomorrow, but, if you have some energy, take a walk along RiverPlace, the shopping and dining esplanade adjacent to your hotel and running along the Willamette waterfront. Most stores will be closed at this time of night, but you'll likely enjoy the window-shopping opportunities as well as an after dinner glass of wine at Thirst Wine Bar (315 SW Montgomery; 503–295–2747).

SATURDAY

8:00 AM

SUNNY SIDE UP

Now that the lights are on so-to-speak, walk from your hotel along RiverPlace until you come to the Little River Café (315 SW Montgomery Street, Suite 310; 503–227–2327), which will provide you with a quick, cheap, and tasty breakfast complete with great outdoor seating at the river's bank.

9:00 AM

TOP OF THE MORNING AT THE BOTTOM

Right there at RiverPlace, just a few steps from where you

nibbled your last bite of breakfast, is Portland Kayak Company (RiverPlace Marina; 503–229–0551). So the next step of renting yourself a kayak should be pretty obvious. (Call for reservations.) Then, push off from the bank and paddle to Oaks Bottom Wildlife Refuge (SE 7th & Sellwood Blvd).

A birdwatcher's paradise in the middle of our urban environment (in the eclectic, antiques' heaven that is the neighborhood of Sellwood in fact), Oaks Bottom Wildlife Refuge is a 170 acre complex of meadows, woodlands, and floodplain wetlands that are either home or home away from home to over 100 different species of North American and neotropical birds as well as several amphibians and mammals. There, you will meander your way past a possible Great Blue Heron, the official bird of the city of Portland, or perhaps an osprey or even a bald eagle.

It should be mentioned that by kayak you will only be able to paddle past the refuge, not actually enter it, but still the sights and sounds should be worthwhile. If however your desire is to hike the trails of Oaks Bottom Wildlife Refuge, depending on the number in your party, you may elect to bring your watercraft to the beach and have someone watch over them while you enter the park. Or you may decide to forego the kayak altogether and simply walk from your hotel across the Hawthorne Bridge and hook up with the Springwater Corridor which functions as one of the refuge's two trails.

The kayak may be rented as early as 9:00, but walking allows you to enter the park at dawn (or anytime after its official opening hour of 5:00) for maximum birdwatching. Also, beginning at 9:00 you may rent a bike at nearby Waterfront Bicycle Rentals (10 SW Ash, Suite 100; 503–227–

1719) and follow the same Springwater Corridor path. Then lock up the bike at Oaks Amusement Park (7805 SE Oaks Park Way; 503–233–5777). Oaks Park is directly accessible from the Springwater Corridor. It's difficult to miss and certainly a handy place to drop off your bike to be able to take on the Wildlife Refuge's other trail, which allows foot traffic only.

However, if kayaking is the way you want to go—and you have means by which to transport the kayak—another tremendous option is Sauvie Island (503–621–3049). Located 15 minutes northwest of Portland, Sauvie Island has a considerable birding reputation, and the 12,000 acres of wildlife area, open April through September, may also be explored by foot. Of course, if you're a birder you know that birdwatching opportunities fluctuate with the seasons, so plan your stay in the Northwest accordingly.

A leisurely kayaking paddle to Oaks Bottom Wildlife Refuge should take about ninety minutes or so, making a round trip of three hours. A hike or a bike ride could vary the timeframe considerably. The following times are thus approximate and are really up to you and how quickly you wish to progress through the preceding.

12:30 PM

A BITE OF NATURE

After you've returned your kayak (or bike) take a walk eight blocks west through downtown to the portion of the South Park Blocks that form the campus of Portland State University. There you will find on Saturday mornings between

8:30–2:00, April through December, the fabulous Portland Farmers Market. With over a hundred different vendors selling fresh produce from A–Z in addition to fresh meat, cut flowers, honey, nuts, eggs, cheese, bread (you get the idea) to over 14,000 people on any given Saturday, you could say this event is on drugs—but then it couldn't be certified organic.

Visit the various vendors and pick up whichever produce has you salivating as well as lunch from any one of the fabulous food carts, such as Basha's for Mediterranean fare and the best falafels west of the Holy Land.

2:00 PM

OVER THE FOREST AND THROUGH THE WOODS

Portland's Washington Park is Disneyland for nature lovers. Among its multiple offerings is the World Forestry Center (4033 SW Canyon; 503–228–1367), which is a nonprofit educational institution dedicated to informing the people of the planet about their forests for the obvious sustainable benefit.

Tour the center's 20,000 square foot Discovery Museum, housing exhibits focused on the forests of the Northwest as well as virtual tours that simulate transportation modes like the Trans-Siberian Railway and a Chinese tour boat in order to investigate boreal, temperate, subtropical, and tropical forest types.

4:00 PM

THE REAL DEAL

Few places on earth offer the type of climate able to host the huge variety of tree and plant life found in the collection at Hoyt Arboretum (4000 SW Fairview Blvd; 503–865–8733). Located in Arlington Heights, just two miles west of downtown Portland and right next door to the World Forestry Center, Hoyt Arboretum boasts over 21 trails covering 12 miles woven between 8000 trees and plants, representing over 1000 species from all around the world in a collection largely arranged in family groups. So, for example, you'll find all the redwoods in a one area and all the maples, currently being considered for inclusion in a worldwide maple conservation effort, in another.

The Visitors Center offers maps for their one, two, and four mile hikes as well as pamphlets explaining a bit about taxonomy and leading you to individual trees and shrubs. The center closes at 3:00, but you can also get much of the above information either from their website, listed at the end of this chapter, or just outside their door. Then hit any one of the trails and take in this "200 acre living museum" where "nature is the oldest of the performing arts."

6:30 PM

ALTERNATATIVE SOURCE REFUEL

You've had a packed day so far, and chances are your jets are running a little low. So make your way back down the Washington Park hill, where you'll find on NW 23rd Avenue a long row of stores, restaurants, bars, and coffee shops. This is Portland's Nob Hill neighborhood. And unless you find another dining option along the way that interests you more, which is not exactly unthinkable considering the glut available, you need to walk or drive north on NW 23rd Avenue through the alphabet ordered streets until you arrive at Thurman. There, just a few paces to the west on NW 23rd Place (not Avenue) is the culinary adventure of Patanegra (1818 NW 23rd Place; 503–227–7282).

Specializing in creative tapas and small plates, Patanegra should have a number of inventive flavor combinations that call to you. If you're with a friend, order several small plates and share. And don't forget to ask the wait staff for a recommendation on one of their yummy wines. If you're lucky, they'll confer with the owner who will likely uncork the right bottle at the right price.

8:30 PM

ROCK THE NIGHT AWAY

Not that you're being profiled, but chances are if you're a wildlife enthusiast you're used to getting up with the Chestnut-backed Chickadees, and you're not exactly looking to go clubbing. So tonight, rock on a slightly different way. Head back to your hotel and get down—that is, by sitting on one of the rocking chairs on the terrace of River-Place Hotel. From this vantage point, you may quietly enjoy the sights and sounds of the river as well as an opportunity to people watch as you rock steady with an after dinner tonic from the bar.

SUNDAY

5:30 AM

EARLY BIRD GETS THE COFFEE

For a hundred years, the Nob Hill Pharmacy was dispensing remedies the old fashioned way. But less than two years ago, the iconic institution immortalized in Gus Van Sant's *Drugstore Cowboy* was transformed into a 24/7 pit stop. Now called Nob Hill Old Pharmacy Café (2100 NW Glisan; 503–548–4049), this appetite apothecary fuels everyone from students cramming for credits to the pre-hangover crowd with all day and all night relief for whatever ails—as long as the diagnosis isn't anything more critical than a chronic case of the munchies. At this time of the morning, you'll be able to find coffee, bagels and lox, scones, croissants and the like. They're currently working on getting their eggs and bacon on for real, so you might luck out if a heavier breakfast is what you're jonesing for.

6:00 AM

SANCTUARY

Amazingly not far from downtown in the neighborhood of Forest Park, the Audubon Society of Portland (5151 NW Cornell Rd; 503–292–6855) offers four miles of forested hiking trails in their nature sanctuary that is home to a mixed conifer forest as well as a stand of Douglas Firs. In addition, Balch Creek there hosts native Cutthroat Trout, and the pond has several amphibians thriving.

But this early in the morning, you're here to see the birds—possibly Steller's Jays, Mourning Doves—the list goes on. And if you care for an even longer hike, the Audubon Society is nestled up against Forest Park (NW 29th Avenue and Upshur to Newberry Road; 503–823–PLAY), and its Wildwood Trail is accessible from the sanctuary.

8:30 AM

GOT VEGAN?

Again, far be it from us to profile, but just on the off chance that you, a nature lover, wildlife enthusiast, might also be a vegetarian, or let's just say "health conscious," we thought we'd throw you a tofurky bone. Veganopolis (412 SW 4th Avenue; 503–226–3400) has an on-the-go bag of vegan jerky or "Vegan Cheetos" to sell you, or, if you've worked up more of an appetite, they have every creative vegan version of your forgotten favorites imaginable. Even the ol' grinder and reuben have been reconfigured seitan style.

9:30 AM

HUNTING FOR HERITAGE

This is the kind of town we are. Portland's Heritage Tree ordinance calls for the Portland City Forester to compile a list every year of the trees that have special importance to the city based on their age, size, type, historical association, or horticultural value. And guess what? These lists are available to you by year, by species, and by location. Just go to the Portland Parks' website (listed at the end of this chapter) for a list and map and then go hunting.

This is a great opportunity to gaze upon trees that a city absolutely enmeshed in trees finds priceless, and it is an entertaining way to get to know Portland. You will of course also require a city map to complement the website's maps which are divided into directional areas. If you think you'll have time and energy for the final suggested activities following the hunt, then choose the map areas on the way toward SW Millikan Way as that is the next stop on the course.

11:30 AM

HABITAT MOSAIC

The Tualatin Hills Nature Park (15655 SW Millikan Way 503–629–6350) is a varied, 219-acre urban greenspace where plant types grow in small patches, similar to the tiles in a mosaic. As animals often require more than one habitat type for their various lifecycle needs, the mosaic tends to cater more realistically to their well-being.

Stop at the Visitors Center and grab a flora and bird checklist. Tualatin Hills Nature Park has marshes, ponds, creeks, meadows, forested wetlands, and forested uplands in addition to paved and unpaved trails, so, whatever you're in the mood for, this mosaic should cater to you as well.

1:30 PM

FORE!

After everything we put you through this weekend, you deserve to treat yourself to what we feel is a truly fine restaurant in this part of town. The Stockpot Broiler (8200 SW Scholls Ferry Road; 503–643–5451) serves classic northwest cuisine as well as comfort food. And you may enjoy your lunch in the elegant dining room, in the bar, or, if the weather is nice, on the outside patio.

The Stockpot is located on a golf course, and its ribbon of green rolls before you accordingly. This may be a slightly more manicured expression of nature than you've been used to during the last couple of days, but now's not the time for roughing it. Hair down, feet up—just allow yourself to stop and smell the bisque.

Important Side Note: As is the case with most of this book, much of the current chapter has assumed the peak weather conditions as well as dawn and dusk times of summer. If there are certain birds, for example, that interest you more than the ones typically seen in Portland in the summer months, you may elect to visit at a different time of year. Most of the same parks, wildlife areas, and activities will still be available, unless otherwise noted, but the preceding hypothetical itinerary will, of course, vary greatly.

Because both nest in the area, great blue herons and bald eagles are here year round. Bald eagles may seem more common in winter because they group up to roost together. And it is true that once spring arrives some leave for other territories, and fewer are left as local nesters. The nest sites are usually along the Columbia River (Sauvie Island and on down to the mouth at Astoria). Osprey also nest here, particularly in Oaks Bottom.

Other birds here during the summer include Anna's hummingbirds, song sparrows, Bewick's wrens, ruby-crowned kinglets, golden-crowned kinglets, bushtits, yellow-rumped warblers, Townsend's warblers, brown creepers, hermit thrushes, American goldfinches, lesser goldfinches, and various swallows to name a few.

As is the case with other chapters, all recommended locations and activities are either located in Portland or are very close in proximity. If however you wish to venture further, the options to enjoy the nature of the Northwest are only as limited as your time and desire. The waterfalls of the Columbia Gorge, the salmon ladder at Bonneville Dam, kayaking in Skomakawa—your trip can conceivably go anywhere.

Also, for the serious birder or just someone who wants to see a sight that is impossible to describe, a planned trip during the roosting of the Vaux's Swifts in the chimney of Chapman School in Portland's northwest (1445 NW 26th Avenue) is highly recommended. Every year the migrating swifts roost in that chimney, and it has become the largest in the world. The exact dates this occurs are up to the swifts, but it always happens in September and lasts for two to three weeks. Contact the Audubon Society of Portland (5151 NW Cornell Rd; 503–292–6895) for more information. And then be sure to make the trip because just after sunset, right before dark, you will witness more than 35,000 swifts flying in to settle for the night in the chimney. This is an event where people bring a date, their family, and friends as well as a picnic and wine to take in a sight that is something akin to watching the chimney vacuum the sky free of birds.

The Skinny

Lay Your Head

Camping Options
www.oregon.gov/OPRD/PARKS/camping.shtml;
www.oregoncitylink.com/portland/camping.htm;
http://gorp.away.com
RiverPlace Hotel 1510 SW Harbor Way; 800–227–1333;
www.riverplacehotel.com

Cool Your Heels

Little River Café 315 SW Montgomery Street, Suite 310;
503–227–2327
Nob Hill Old Pharmacy Café 2100 NW Glisan; 503–548–4049
Patanegra 1818 NW 23rd Place; 503–227–7282
Stockpot Broiler 8200 SW Scholls Ferry Road; 503–643–5451; www.stockpotbroiler.com
Thirst Wine Bar 315 SW Montgomery; 503–295–2747;
www.thirstwinebar.com
Three Degrees 1510 SW Harbor Way; 503–295–6166;
http://www.riverplacehotel.com/restaurant.html
Veganopolis 412 SW 4th Avenue; 503–226–3400;
www.veganopolis.com

Actions Speak Louder Than Words

40–Mile Loop www.40mileloop.org
Audubon Society of Portland 5151 NW Cornell Rd; 503–292–6855; www.audubonportland.org
Forest Park NW 29th Avenue and Upshur to Newberry Road; 503–823–PLAY; www.portlandonline.com/parks; www.greentrailsmaps.com
Heritage Tree Hunting www.portlandonline.com/parks/index.cfm?c=eacia
Hoyt Arboretum 4000 SW Fairview Blvd; 503–865–8733; www.hoytarboretum.org
Oaks Amusement Park 7805 SE Oaks Park Way; 503–233–5777; www.oakspark.com
Oaks Bottom Wildlife Refuge SE 7th & Sellwood Blvd; www.portlandparks.org
Portland Farmers Market 503–241–0032; www.portlandfarmersmarket.org
Sauvie Island 503–621–3049; www.sauvieisland.org
Smith and Bybee Lakes Wildlife Area www.smithandbybeelakes.org
Springwater Corridor www.40mileloop.org/trail_springwatercorridor.htm
Tualatin Hills Nature Park 15655 SW Millikan Blvd; 503–629–6350; www.thprd.org
Vaux's Swifts at the Chapman School Chimney 1445 NW 26th Avenue; 503–292–6895; www.audubonportland.org
World Forestry Center 4033 SW Canyon; 503–228–1367; www.worldforestrycenter.org

Get It In Gear

Portland Kayak Company RiverPlace Marina; 503–229–0551; www.portlandrivercompany.com
Waterfront Bicycle Rentals 10 SW Ash, Suite 100; 503–227–1719; www.waterfrontbikes.net

Check Under the 'Hood

Arlington Heights
www.portlandneighborhood.com/arlingtonheights.html

Downtown
www.portlandneighborhood.com/downtown–portland.html

Forest Park
www.portlandneighborhood.com/forestpark.html

Nob Hill
www.portlandneighborhood.com/nobhill.html

Sellwood
www.portlandneighborhood.com/sellwood–moreland.html

St. Johns
www.portlandneighborhood.com/stjohns.html

Family Weekend

Oaks Amusement Park

T he fodder for jokes, the subject of comedies and their sequels starring Chevy Chase, and an excuse for at least one really good fight, the phenomenon known as the family vacation can be a treacherous combination of different ages with different interests and abilities in addition to obligatory doses of kid-centric activities seemingly designed to bore the one brain cell required for parental involvement. Add to this an unexpected bout of naughtiness or a nap not taken, and you've got the best laid plans of mice and children.

Of course, Portland can't guarantee that filial fiascos won't take place within its borders. But this city offers so many unique, interesting, and fun family friendly options, many of them wherein several levels of skill and interest can be accommodated at once, that younger ones of the family will likely be too occupied and amazed to bother building a disaster.

Therefore, let's get busy before any mischief-makers notice that Portland's got a really good plan.

FRIDAY

6:00 PM

BACK TO SCHOOL

The kids might be on vacation. You've long since graduated. But on this trip, you're all headed back to class. Part of the local string of McMenamins hotels, restaurants, breweries, concert venues, and movie theaters, Kennedy School (5736 NE 33rd Avenue; 888–249–3983) is one of Portland's most prized unique spaces. An actual former elementary school located in the Concordia neighborhood and dating back to 1915, Kennedy School has been transformed into a hugely successful lodging establishment with amazing amenities for everyone in your clan.

For starters, each classroom has been divided into two guestrooms complete with original chalkboards and cloak-rooms and even their own names derived from former teachers or nursery rhymes with inspired artwork to match the theme. So where children once rested their heads on desks, you will now rest yours on a queen-sized bed. Depending on how many little students are stowing away with you, up to two rollaway beds can fit in each room, or you may wish to split up and attend the class next door.

There will nearly always be an activity available that calls to at least someone in your party. So anytime some-one's too cranky, tired, or "playful" for an item on the itinerary, there will be plenty to fall back on at Kennedy School. You'll find the onsite movie theater (admission to which is free for your entire stay) in what was once the old auditorium, concerts, even live radio theatre on occasion, a soaking pool where once was the teacher's lounge, the Courtyard Restaurant in the old cafeteria that now serves delish McMenamins pub fare, the Honors Bar for parents with halos, the Detention Bar for those who'd rather smoke there than sneak one in the bathroom, and homemade beer, beer, beer. In sum, you're checking into a study on what school was supposed to prepare us to do in the first place—use our imagination.

7:00 PM

GOES TOGETHER LIKE

Peanut Butter & Ellie's (4405 SW Vermont; 503–282–1783) is so experienced at "redefining family dining" that they hold workshops on how to open your own similar business. But tonight you're here to feed your kids something healthy and feed yourself something more interesting than the typical family restaurant staples of pizza and fried everything.

At PB & Ellie's, there is a strong emphasis on organic, locally raised, and sustainable. They understand that kids eat with their eyes first, so their homemade organic peanut butter with jelly sandwiches are shaped like hearts. A salad might come served in a tipped over bucket, and for breakfast a waffle will be shaped like a farm animal. Adults have such items as flatiron steak, harvest chicken, and ribs to choose from while little guys can pick anything from a "Burrito Bus" to a grilled sandwich of S'mores, peanut butter, marshmallows, and chocolate chips.

The owners claim that every detail of the restaurant has been, "carefully explored from the perspective of children and their adults," and they even organize special events like pajama concerts, family dinner theatre, and themed dinner menus following local librarian presented storytimes. They've also devised a clever way to get kids to explore further out the culinary limb by creating a "Picky Eater Insurance" program that replaces a more adventurous choice with an expedited plan B like peanut butter and jelly or grilled cheese should junior be of a changeable mind.

121

8:30 PM

DIFFERENT STROKES

Miniature golf to bumper boats, laser tag to go karts, a "Kidopolis Playland" of five levels of soft play area for those under five feet, and two floors with over 150 arcade and prize redemption games—Family Fun Center south of Portland in Wilsonville (29111 SW Town Center Loop W.; 503–685–5000) has fun for just about all the different ways your family can spell it. In addition, the onsite Bullwinkle's Restaurant serves burgers, sandwiches, salads, wraps, and ice cream in case you decide to forego the earlier restaurant entry and just dive right into play mecca mode.

So, no matter which page each person in your party happens to be on at the moment, Family Fun Center's 24,000 square feet of options—and that's just inside—should have an enticing chapter of amusement.

SATURDAY

8:00 AM

HALL PASS

You've got a packed day ahead, so take the hassle free option of heading down the hall to breakfast at Kennedy School's Courtyard Restaurant. Beginning at 7:00, they serve biscuits and gravy to smoked salmon scrambles and Amaretto French toast, plus a Bloody Mary, Screwdriver, or Greyhound in case the kid-focused day ahead has you wanting to buttress yourself with a little liquid fortification.

9:30 AM

PLEASE TOUCH THE EXHIBITS

The Portland Children's Museum (4015 SW Canyon Road; 503–223–6500) isn't the kind of place where scary red velvet ropes steer you and your child like cultural cattle away from all the cool stuff. Instead, youngsters are encouraged to dive right in and engage wholeheartedly in interactive, educational exhibits that teach clay and sculpture, water dynamics, wellness basics, the nuts and bolts of construction, and much more.

In this hands-on extravaganza, kids may panel a wall and connect the plumbing in a 17-foot-high, two-story house or climb inside a mini-ambulance as another child operates the emergency dispatch center. Your little theatre arts aficionados can stage a production by operating lighting and sound boards or by going backstage and controlling the curtain. Or maybe your kid is the type drawn to nab the director's chair. Children may dig in a pit of rubber "gravel." Babies and toddlers can crawl though a multi-sensory mock forest. They may even enjoy squishing and squeezing clay as older ones learn to sculpt.

In other words, their minds busy, their hands dirty, kids visiting the Portland Children's Museum engage in hours of delightful playtime while garnering life skills training and artistic, cultural experience. Watch out daytime television.

12:00 PM

MONKEY BARS

No need even to get in the car for your next adventure. Right there in the Arlington Heights neighborhood, next to where your child dug, hammered, tried on costumes backstage, and peered at hair, bugs, and skin under a microscope at the Portland Children's Museum is the Oregon Zoo (4001 SW Canyon Road; 503–226–1561).

Dating back 120 years, the zoo remains Oregon's leading paid attraction, it's exhibits ranging from an African rainforest and savanna to the tundra of Alaska, a flooded forest of the Amazon, Black Bear Ridge, and Eagle Canyon to name not even one quarter of the habitats presented. Three trains (one of them seasonal) offer scenic excursions in the zoo and the forests of Washington Park when little legs grow weary. And when hungry stomachs begin to roar louder than the inmates, the Cascade Grill Restaurant offers sit down dining, and AfriCafe, Black Rhino, and BearWalk Café offer quicker on-the-go options like hamburgers, hot dogs, and pizza.

3:00 PM

EVEN LITTLE COWGIRLS GET TO SNOOZE

Big morning so far, so if your preference is to enjoy the remainder of the day instead of dealing with cranky fallout, might want to head back to the hotel for some much-deserved R&R. And because you're staying at Kennedy School, now any older kids who outgrew napping about the same moment that storytime lost its charm have plenty to do while you and the wee ones rest. Or maybe the ages of your brood will allow you to grab a beer at one of the bars down the hall or maybe a matinee—or both at the same time. Yup, such behavior is only given a gold star at this school.

4:30 PM

FUN AND GAMES

One of the oldest continuously running amusement parks in the entire United States sits on the eastern bank of the Willamette River in the Portland neighborhood of Sellwood. Dating back to 1905, Oaks Amusement Park (7805 SE Oaks Park Way; 503–233–5777) has managed to maintain a measure of bygone era charm. That said, much of the ride area will not evoke a nostalgic sense of Main Street Americana with Robert Preston singing about his 76 trombones. Aside from the historic Dance Pavilion and the traditional wooden roller skating rink complete with live Wurlitzer accompaniment on Wednesdays and Sundays, much of the park smacks more of a carnival. But somewhere between the park's giant namesake oaks, the grass, the river, a tiny train that meanders around the above, and rides like the Looping Thunder Roller Coaster and Scream-N-Eagle—that won't steal your day in Imagineered serpentine lines of endless proportions—is a refreshing, navigable throwback in which your kids will spend their time having a blast instead of waiting for one.

7:30 PM

THIS ONE'S FOR YOU

By now, if you see another corn dog, waffle cone, or pastel of cotton candy, you'll lose what's left of your appetite. But never fear, those little stomachs of steel accompanying you will find plenty to occupy their mouths and time with—while you find a delicious, mature culinary experience—at Laurelwood Public House and Brewery (5115 NE Sandy; 503–282–0622) in the neighborhood of Rose City Park.

An adult establishment that also happens to be very kid friendly, Laurelwood offers two play areas and a menu where each child's entrée, such as spaghetti marinara or chicken strips, comes with ice cream and a drink. With the Portland emphasis on fresh, local, sustainable, and organic, Laurelwood dishes the more mature palate such choices as chicken breasts topped with artichoke and bacon stuffing, organic free-range red barbeque ribs, and bouillabaisse. And if that weren't enough, as their name might have clued you in, Laurelwood makes its own multi-award-winning beer, a couple of which are even certified organic. Cheers!

9:30 PM

GO DOWN SWINGING

In case someone in your party is just not ready to give up on the day and call it a night, again the hotel has plenty to keep you busy as long as another someone is available to remain in the room and supervise the surrendered.

SUNDAY

8:30 AM

AS AMERICAN AS APPLE PANCAKES

A family business in its second and third generation as well as a national breakfast phenomenon, The Original Pancake House (8601 SW 24th Avenue; 503–246–9007) was founded right here in Portland over a half-century ago. There is no promise of a playroom here, but, with signature items like the apple pancakes and the baked, air filled Dutch Baby, the restaurant's sugary morning delights should be enough to keep little ones entertained without plastic toy accoutrements.

10:00 AM

INDUSTRIOUS MINDS WANT TO KNOW

One of the nation's top ten science museums, the Oregon Museum of Science and Industry (1945 SE Water Avenue; 800–955–OMSI) is nothing less than a playground for your child's brain. Right on the banks of the Willamette River in the Hosford-Abernathy neighborhood, the museum's exhibition space and science labs cover 219,000 square feet of youth centered, interactive education. In addition, the museum boasts the Northwest's largest planetarium, a five-story OMNIMAX domed theater, and the star of *The Hunt for Red October*, the USS Blueback which was America's last non-nuclear, fast attack submarine, now available for tours and even sleepovers.

And don't worry, big kids such as yourself should find much to explore and investigate, likely discovering in the process just how many classes you must have ditched. So while your child's going hands on with chemistry, technology, and physics, you'll be getting in touch with your inner Hawking. And when all of you find that mass caloric units of energy are deficient, the onsite OMSI café should be able to provide the corresponding solution.

1:30 PM

CURIOUS GORGE

For an informative trek through the Columbia Gorge as well as a river tour of awesome proportions, take one of the Narrated Sightseeing Excursions aboard the Columbia Gorge Sternwheeler (800–224–3901). From May through October, the 2:00 cruise boards at 1:30 in Marine Park located in Cascade Locks, Oregon, which is 45 minutes east of Portland off Interstate 84. (Reservations are of course recommended.)

Riding on an authentic triple-deck paddle wheeler, which itself is an excursion, older ears may cue into accounts of the Lewis and Clark expedition, the Oregon Trail, Bridge of the Gods, and riverboats while eyes of all ages will feast on the immense beauty of the second longest river in the country and the grand gorge that cradles it.

OR...

...if the time of day is inconvenient for an adventure such as a river tour, Columbia Gorge Sternwheeler certainly offers other cruise times and options, even a Sunday Brunch Cruise. However, if the tone of the activity is larger than what you were anticipating or the weather is not cooperating, a lovely alternative is certainly the Family Drop-In Sundays available downtown at the Portland Art Museum (1219 SW Park Avenue; 503–226–0973). Here kids are welcome to drop by for as little as just a few minutes or as long as they like anytime between 1:00 and 3:00 on Sunday afternoons for artmaking activities with local artists, instructors, and museum educators. (No need to register for this, but timed tickets are required and available in advance.)

Also, the Portland Regional Arts and Culture Council lists the scoop on several other artistic, cultural, and educational activities for youth such as the Northwest Film Center's film club for teens and Family Discovery Sundays at the Museum of Contemporary Craft. Just check out these websites at the end of this chapter for more information.

5:00 PM

AND THEY ALL LIVED HAPPILY EVER AFTER

Old Wives' Tales (1300 E Burnside; 503–238–0470) provides three different dining rooms, the main one adjoining to a children's playroom for toddlers on up to 10-year-olds. Located in the Buckman neighborhood, Old Wives' Tales features multi-ethnic, vegetarian friendly fare with an emphasis on fresh and preservative free. The menu caters creatively to young ones with such lunch and dinner offerings as noodles, asiago cheese and cream, rosemary chicken sandwiches, and sesame roasted yams. But they

129

can tone it down for more finicky palates with such standards as bean and cheese burritos, grilled cheese, or peanut butter and jelly sandwiches. For adults, kick that up to an Indian burrito with savory red lentil tomato dal or Greek spanokopita or even Southwestern chicken phyllo pastries.

Now, while the kids are enmeshed in either their playtime or their plate, take a few moments before heading home to relax, refuel, regroup and—because of Portland—rethink the family vacation.

The Skinny

Lay Your Head

Kennedy School 5736 NE 33rd Avenue; 888–249–3983; www.mcmenamins.com

Cool Your Heels

Laurelwood Public House and Brewery 5115 NE Sandy; 503–282–0622; www.laurelwoodbrewpub.com
Old Wives' Tales 1300 E Burnside; 503–238–0470; www.oldwivestalesrestaurant.com
Original Pancake House 8601 SW 24th Avenue; 503–246–9007; www.originalpancakehouse.com
Peanut Butter & Ellie's 4405 SW Vermont; 503–282–1783; www.pbecafe.com

Actions Speak Louder Than Words

Columbia Gorge Sternwheeler Marine Park in Cascade Locks; 800–224–3901; www.sternwheeler.com
Family Discovery Sundays at the Museum of

Contemporary Craft 724 NW Davis; 503–223–2654; www.museumofcontemporarycraft.org; www.racc.org/artseducation/events.php
Family Drop-In Sundays at the Portland Art Museum 1219 SW Park Avenue; 503–226–0973; www.portlandartmuseum.org; www.racc.org/artseducation/events.php
Family Fun Center in Wilsonville 29111 SW Town Center Loop W.; 503–685–5000; www.fun–center.com
Northwest Film Center's Film Club for Teens 503–221–1156; www.nwfilm.org; www.racc.org/artseducation/events.php
Oaks Amusement Park 7805 SE Oaks Park Way; 503–233–5777; www.oakspark.com
Oregon Museum of Science and Industry 1945 SE Water Avenue; 800–955–OMSI; www.omsi.edu
Oregon Zoo 4001 SW Canyon Road; 503–226–1561; www.oregonzoo.org
Portland Children's Museum 4015 SW Canyon Road; 503–223–6500; www.portlandcm.org
Regional Arts & Culture Council 108 NW 9th Avenue; 503-823-5111; www.racc.org

Check Under the 'Hood

Arlington Heights
www.portlandneighborhood.com/arlingtonheights.html

Buckman
www.portlandneighborhood.com/buckman.html

Concordia
www.portlandneighborhood.com/concordia.html

Downtown
www.portlandneighborhood.com/downtown–portland.html

Hosford–Abernathy
www.portlandneighborhood.com/hosford–abernathy.html

Rose City Park
www.portlandneighborhood.com/rosecitypark.html

Sellwood
www.portlandneighborhood.com/sellwood–moreland.html

Sports Weekend

PGE Park

Though ridiculed and misunderstood, true spectator sports fans know on some level of their being that what they're watching is really a metaphor for life. The seemingly ceaseless aiming of one's energy toward a goal, the role of teamwork and comradery, the value of a home base—all speak to the need to see our own story told through larger than life heroes and heroines in concise narrative bouts of triumph and defeat.

And though our legends and legend makers live on—perhaps the main reason for telling and retelling the fable in the first place—we're never fully able to spin the tale of our ability to beat back, harness, and control nature, try as we may. We mow to artistic perfection the fields that serve as our heroes' stages. We draw meticulous white lines, marking meaningful boundaries with near atomic precision. But we are yet unable even to stutter nature from its course. Our quarterbacks retire. The lawns grow, erasing our artwork.

And the season comes to an end.

So it is in the cyclical nature of sports that we recognize perhaps their strongest life parallel. One season ends. The next one begins. For this reason it is impossible to catch all of one's favorite sports at any one time or over any one weekend. That is why, for this chapter only, we have compiled a composite weekend. In other words, the following itinerary is actually unfeasible due to the nature of each sport's season.

Instead, however, this particular chapter is meant to inform the visiting fan as to the abundance of spectator sport options available in Portland, their traditions and meaning within the community as well as their season parameters.

Now, play ball!

FRIDAY

6:00 PM

A PLACE TO HANG YOUR CAP

For the most part, the attempt of this book has been to define and present the quintessential Portland weekend experience, one that cannot be easily duplicated anywhere else in the world. Because of this, businesses and services that have companion chain locations in other parts of the country have been almost entirely excluded from these chapters. However, for several reasons an exception will be made for the Portland Marriott Downtown Waterfront Hotel (1401 SW Naito Pkwy; 503–226–7600).

First, it should be mentioned that, although Marriott is a recognizable corporate entity with room availability practically on the moon, this particular Marriott is a prominent fixture of our iconic downtown skyline and, as such, has woven itself into the daily visual landscape that we call home. Secondly, this hotel simply offers unparalleled views of the Willamette River, Portland's eastside and, weather permitting, the majesty that is Mt. Hood. Thirdly, every single one of the following sporting events, bars, restaurants, and activities lie within walking distance from this hotel or are easily reached via Portland's tremendous

TriMet public transportation system, which itself is likewise simply accessed from the hotel. Plain fact of the matter is, if you stay at this hotel, you will never need a car to reach any of the scheduled destinations during your entire stay. And finally, undoubtedly no small reason for the rabid sports fan you are, you're staying at the Portland Marriott Downtown Waterfront Hotel because of Champions Restaurant and Sports Bar (503–499–6393).

Right above the lobby with a few of its own nice views of the river, Champions will serve as your in-house sports bar all weekend long. They offer over 20 screens, DirectTV satellite, and broadcast packages for all major professional sports, so you'll never be far away from that game you thought you'd have to miss because you're on the road plus any downtime game time opportunities. In addition, they serve several of our famous local brews, and much of the staff such as the wise and friendly barkeeps have been there a long time and are pure Portland through and through.

So check in, hang your cap, wear one of the others you brought (we know you packed a few), and get your game on.

7:00 PM

JOIN THE ARMY

The Timber Army is the horde of die-hard, fanatical fans of the Portland Timbers professional soccer team who sits behind the north goal dressed in team green complete with matching scarves. Led by a roaring chainsaw, the Army shouts, screams, blows their soccer horns, and chants incessantly while the team plays, just like it's done in Europe.

Not all of the synchronized songs are exactly on-color, so if you like to keep the little one's ears from such symphonies, you might want to aim your tickets toward the sidelines, but be aware that the Army makes itself heard wherever you are. As raucous as it sounds, it's all in good fun, and, in fact, if you made it to town a little early, a pre-game trip to where the Timber Army assembles its ranks and imbibes near the stadium is a good time and recommended: The Bullpen (1730 SW Taylor; 503–222–3063).

Formally part of the North American Soccer League in the '70s and '80s, the Timbers reformed in 2001 with the United Soccer League, first division. The team, not to mention the Army, proceeded to enjoy a stunning five-year winning streak before hitting a speed bump in 2006. But in 2007, a defender who had played each of the five winning seasons brought some fresh legs to the coaching position, and the team's been forming their counter attack.

The season for the Portland Timbers (1844 SW Morrison; Tickets: 503–553–5555) runs from approximately early April to early September, with the majority of home start times at 7:00.

Of course, any dyed-in-the-wool sports fan fuels much of his or her passion from the energy of the actual stadium. The right park will just make you feel the right way. PGE Park (1844 SW Morrison; 503–553–5400) is that park. Built in 1893, it's not the largest, but it remains grand and handsome and plays its own role in any event.

140

Originally called Multnomah Field, PGE Park is a sports sanctuary in the bustle of downtown Portland's next door neighbor, Goose Hollow. In its long and storied lifetime, the stadium has hosted presidents Taft and Harding, witnessed Elvis, Bowie, and Bob Hope as well as a fire that began in the Exposition Building on the field's northern border. As this was the largest wooden structure west of the Mississippi at the time, the conflagration wound up destroying seven city blocks and melting the steel girders on the park's grandstands, of course requiring reconstruction.

History aside, PGE Park is a highly negotiable breath of fresh air. First of all, though parking remains a strikeout, the park is located right on the TriMet Max line, so access requires no driving and pitifully little walking. Lines may form at some of the larger concession stands, but if you're willing to take a few extra steps, a lesser occupied stand is likely to be found. They offer the usual stadium fare but in addition supplement with high-end craft brews and an exceptionally nice beer garden run by the Widmer Brothers that offers hamburgers and even salmon fresh off an outdoor grill as well as a full bar and table seating—right on the field—accessible with nothing more than a general admission ticket.

9:30 PM

BATTER UP

On Deck Sports Bar and Grill (910 NW 14th Avenue; 503–227–7020) has 20 HDTVs and 4 big screen plasmas positioned around its rather chic sports viewing venue in Portland's hip Pearl District. Grab a seat "courtside" (the bar), "midfield" (open tables), or in one of the "box seats" (booths) and take in several games while getting some serious face time with the restaurant's "something for everyone" menu featuring burgers, sandwiches, wraps, salads, fish and chips, and more.

SATURDAY

9:00 AM

A RIVER'S WAKE

It's likely not every morning that outside your door lies a sports track etched into a river. Admittedly it's not every morning in Portland either, but the Willamette does go to sport often. The most famous sporting events that occur on the Willamette River are the Dragon Boat Races, a tradition that has seen great partnership between Portland and its sister city in Taiwan, Kaohsiung City, ROC, including even the gifting to Portland from China of several of these spectacular vessels.

Dragon Boat races always highlight the Portland Rose Festival in June. However, there are a couple other race dates on the Willamette. Visit the Dragon Boat websites listed at the end of this chapter for more information.

Further examples of the type of water sport events available on the Willamette River include collegiate and amateur rowing with a combined and overlapping season that runs from February to November. There are also sailing regattas held by Willamette Sailing Club (503–246–5345) on Sunday afternoons in February, March, September, and October if you decide to switch the water sports activity away from Saturday. The public is welcome to watch these races from the Willamette Sailing Club's docks and clubhouse.

11:00 AM

CHEERS ON THE HALF SHELL

Fifty years of friendly service, $1.99 breakfasts all day, a fireplace surrounded by boatloads of TVs playing game after game, their own signature brew called Turtle Dew and cocktails like Turtle Farts, a morning happy hour designed for the stressed out medical staff rappelling off Pill Hill after a shift at nearby Oregon Health Sciences University— all combine to make the Cheerful Tortoise (1939 SW 6th Avenue; 503–224–3377) a memorable downtown must-stop for the AM sports fan.

Chow down on a four egg, build-your-own omelette, ogle your favorite game on one of the astounding 40 HD and satellite televisions and celebrate one of those places where you know it's 5:00 somewhere else, and it makes morning sports' sense to have a beer with your breakfast.

1:30 PM

VIKING COWBOY

In 2007, the city of Portland managed to score two huge points for itself in the national game of prized staff and

143

team member acquisitions. The first was Portland State University's hiring of the famous man-in-black coach himself, Jerry Glanville. Former NFL coach of the Houston Oilers and the Atlanta Falcons, not to mention a national television commentator, Coach Glanville brings his cowboy swagger and unique style to Portland's own Division 1-AA college football team and has promised to "get this thing going 100 mph."

Portland State University Vikings (Tickets: 527 SW Hall Street, Suite 415; 503–725–4000) hold practice at the Community Recreation Field on campus, but games are held at PGE Park (information above under Friday's Portland Timbers' entry).

The Viking football season runs from approximately the first week in September to mid-November, and at home start times are typically 1:30, 2:30, or 6:00.

5:00 PM

PASTTIME'S PAST

Now that you're getting the opportunity to experience a sample of Portland sports today, you'll likely enjoy acquainting yourself with the Oregon sports of yesterday. So take a timeout between the games of the present and get up to speed on the legends that got us here. The State of Oregon Sports Hall of Fame and Museum (321 SW Salmon; 503–227–7466) is an athletics' archive offering 9000 square feet of memories in interactive displays, videos, trophies, uniforms, and more including a gift shop in case you want to take a couple extra moments back home with you.

7:00 PM

BY ANY OTHER NAME

While you're in Portland, the Rose Quarter (Box Office: One Center Court, Suite 100; 877–789–ROSE) will serve as your indoor sports spectator playground. This prized, enormous complex is located in Portland's Lloyd District and comprised of the 12,000 seat Memorial Coliseum, the 6,500 seat Theater of the Clouds, the 40,000 square-foot Exhibit Hall, and the Rose Quarter Commons. Of course, the jewel in the Rose Quarter crown is its largest venue, the Rose Garden Arena at 19,980 seats, and it is home to the NBA's Portland Trail Blazers, the Western Hockey League's Winter Hawks, and the National Lacrosse League's Portland LumberJax as well as many other major indoor events and concerts.

When home during their respective seasons, each of these three professional teams often plays on Saturdays, with typical starts times around 7:00–7:30. The Trail Blazers' (Customer Service: One Center Court; 503–797–9600) schedule runs from October to April. The Winter Hawks (Front Office: Memorial Coliseum, 300 N. Winning Way; Tickets: 503–236–HAWK) play from September to March. And the LumberJax (One Center Court, Suite 150; 503–736–2130) swing steady from December to April. Obviously, as these schedules overlap considerably, if your visit is planned between the months of October and April, you run a very good chance of seeing one or more games played by one or more of these teams:

BLAZERS

As mentioned earlier in the chapter, Portland itself scored two major points for local sports in 2007. The second slam-dunk was beating the odds to nab the 2007 number one pick in the NBA draft. The Trail Blazers chose outstanding Ohio State center, Greg Oden. History is waiting to be made, and the glory of the '77 championship lead by the likes of Bill Walton and Maurice Lucas is waiting to be restored.

WINTER HAWKS

In 1976, Portland became the first American city to host a team in the Western Hockey League, which itself is part of the Canadian Major Junior Hockey League and the number one go to source for America's National Hockey League recruiting. In their thirty-plus years of hitting the ice, the Winter Hawks have racked up numerous pennants and playoff championships and have managed to skate home with the Memorial Cup twice.

LUMBERJAX

In 2005, at the age of 24, Angela Batinovich became the youngest owner of a professional sports team in the US. Arriving on the scene with a background in fashion and her own designer label, Bat's Daughter, no one knew exactly what to expect from her brand new lacrosse team, The LumberJax. One year and a few really smart moves later, Angela was named the 2006 National Lacrosse League Executive of the Year.

Smart move number one, Angela hired a top-notch coach, and then, understanding that not everyone is familiar with the game of lacrosse, she pimped the experience by pumping in loud music and ramping up the atmosphere to that of a stadium party, thus ensuring a good time regardless of spectator experience.

9:30 PM

EXTRA INNINGS

Why let the games end there? You've probably been noshing at games all day, but we know your appetite for sports is insatiable. So for more on the court, on the field, on the rink action, aim the crew toward Claudia's Sports Pub & Grill in the Richmond neighborhood (3006 SE Hawthorne; 503–232–1744). Claudia's has been quenching a thirst for sports and beer since 1958, offering approximately 42 different versions of the latter, and, for the former, all bases are covered with satellite packages like MLB Extra Innings, NFL Sunday Ticket, ESPN Game Plan, NHL Center Ice, NBA League Pass, and Mega March Madness. And just in case your other hunger is not down for the count after an all day stadium fare fest, Claudia's will dish up pizza to burgers to salad until midnight.

However, if you prefer your Saturday night sports bars with a little hip-hop, DJs, and dancing, The City Sportsbar and Restaurant in downtown (424 SW 4th Avenue; 503–221–2489) transforms from game-set-match of a sports spectator venue to nightclub with their Sexy Saturdays events. Here you may or may not be able to see your favorite game on one of the umpteen screens, but there will

147

definitely be some action.

SUNDAY

9:00 AM

BOX SEATS

Many sports bars will serve breakfast during football season, but in Sellwood the small and homey SkyBox Pub & Grill (7995 SE Milwaukie; 503–731–6399) dishes it all year long. In addition, you'll find yourself surrounded by televisions playing a comprehensive array of sporting events via DirectTV in one of Portland's most beloved sports bar settings. And if that weren't enough, the SkyBox website easily links to game schedules, so you'll know what to look for when you get there.

11:00 AM

GOOOOOOOOOAALL!

University of Portland's Pilots (5000 N. Willamette Blvd; 503–943–7525) are one of the finest women's soccer programs in the NCAA. Since the team's inception in 1989, they have made it to the NCAA quarterfinals eleven times. Eleven. In 2002, the Pilots won their first national championship, and in 2005 the Pilots became the second team in women's soccer history to win a national championship following an undefeated season.

The Pilots' season runs from September to December, and all games are played at Harry A. Merlo Field. Located on the University of Portland campus in the University Park neighborhood, Merlo Field has hosted several NCAA playoffs and even international matches as well as national and Olympic training teams, and it is considered one of the finest soccer facilities in the country at any level.

2:00 PM

PEANUTS AND CRACKERJACKS

Sunday afternoons for the Portland summer sports fan are spelled Beavers (Box Office: 1844 SW Morrison; 503–224-4400). Part of the Pacific Coast League, the Portland Beavers are the Triple-A farm club of the San Diego Padres. However, their role in the Portland sports landscape goes back over one hundred years as the Beavers saw their inaugural season in 1903 as the Portland Browns. They were the Giants of 1904 before becoming the Beavers of 1905, and triple-A status was bestowed in 2001.

Beaver season runs from April to September, and all games are held at the equally storied and historic PGE Park.

5:00 PM

SLIDE TOWARD HOME

Pack up all the bobble heads, mini-bats, mini-pennants, and other fan appreciation treasures you've accumulated during your stay and head toward the sidelines before someone at the home office places you on the DL.

The Skinny

Lay Your Head

Portland Marriott Downtown Waterfront Hotel 1401 SW Naito Pkwy; 503–226–7600; www.marriott.com

Cool Your Heels

Bullpen 1730 SW Taylor; 503–222–3063
Champions Restaurant and Sports Bar 1401 SW Naito Pkwy; 503–499–6393; www.marriott.com
Cheerful Tortoise 1939 SW 6th Avenue; 503–224–3377; www.cheerfulgrills.com
City Sportsbar and Restaurant 424 SW 4th Avenue; 503–221–2489; www.citysportsbar.com
Claudia's Sports Pub & Grill 3006 SE Hawthorne; 503–232–1744; www.claudiaspub.com
On Deck Sports Bar and Grill 910 NW 14th Avenue; 503–227–7020; www.ondecksportsbar.com
SkyBox Pub & Grill 7995 SE Milwaukie; 503–731–6399; www.skyboxpub.com

Actions Speak Louder Than Words

Collegiate and Amateur Rowing
www.willamette.edu/athletics/teams/rowing;
www.willametterowing.org; www.oregonrowing.org
Dragon Boat Races www.pksca.com;
www.dragonsports.org; www.wasabiusa.org
PGE Park 1844 SW Morrison; 503–553–5400;
www.pgepark.com
Portland Beavers 1844 SW Morrison; 503–224–4400;
www.portlandbeavers.com
Portland LumberJax One Center Court, Suite 150; 503–
736–2130; www.portlandjax.com
Portland State University Vikings Tickets: 527 SW Hall
Street, Suite 415; 503–725–4000;
www.goviks.com/info/tickets
Portland Timbers 1844 SW Morrison; 503–553–5555;
www.portlandtimbers.com
Portland Trail Blazers Customer Service: One Center
Court; 503–797–9600; www.nba.com/blazers
Portland Winter Hawks Front Office: Memorial Coli-
seum, 300 N. Winning Way; Tickets: 503–236–HAWK;
www.winterhawks.com
Rose Quarter Box Office: One Center Court, Suite 100;
877–789–ROSE; www.rosequarter.com
Sailing Regattas 503–246–5345;
www.willamettesailingclub.com
State of Oregon Sports Hall of Fame and Museum 321
SW Salmon; 503–227–7466; www.oregonsportshall.org
University of Portland Pilots 5000 N. Willamette Blvd;
503–943–7525; www.portlandpilots.com/sports/wsoccer

Check Under the 'Hood

Downtown
www.portlandneighborhood.com/downtown–portland.html

Goose Hollow
www.portlandneighborhood.com/goosehollow.html

Lloyd District
www.portlandneighborhood.com/lloyd.html

Pearl District
www.portlandneighborhood.com/pearldistrict.html

Richmond
www.portlandneighborhood.com/richmond.html

Sellwood
www.portlandneighborhood.com/sellwood–moreland.html

University Park
www.portlandneighborhood.com/universitypark.html

Shopping Weekend

Shopping on 23rd Avenue

R ight out of the bag, if you're looking for directions to the mall, you might just want to skip this chapter. Alas, during this shopping weekend you will not step foot in even one of the homogenous, identical enterprises that are the malls of America. Nope. Plain fact of the matter is, if you're coming to Portland to shop, then what you're ultimately looking for is an eclectic, interesting, unique, and fun time.

Sure, we've got malls. Who doesn't? That's the point. But in Portland, we've also got the kind of fertile, creative atmosphere where a budding entrepreneur will feel right at home to open, say, a shop specializing in supplies for the garden—the type of garden that grows without soil (Urban Flora; 2865 SE Division; 503–236–3344), or an outlet of locally made Jacuzzis designed just for your feet (Ashiyu; 8015 SE 13th Avenue; 503–232–0920), or a showroom of 100-year-old Brazilian timbers organically incorporated into modern furniture (EWF Modern; 1122 NW Glisan; 503–295–7336).

And do we have clothes! But in Portland you'll find so much more than the pop uniform fashioned in a corporate boardroom and rolled out quarterly. That's here too if you want it, but so are locally designed, handmade, socially responsible, one-of-a-kind fashions as well as international runway imports.

So grab your purse, pumps, and plastic—or wallet and walking shoes. First step's the funnest. You've got a shopping disorder, and Portland's got the retail therapy.

FRIDAY

6:00 PM

BASE CAMP

Even a seasoned hunter such as you needs a place to lay up hard won supplies for the night. And practically the only way a hotel for an adventure getaway devoted to pure, unadulterated consumerism could be any more conveniently located to its destination is if it were placed at the customer service counter of this chapter's 4-letter-word. So you'll be resting your head—and dropping off your shopping bags—where you'll be within walking or easily accessed public transit distance to a veritable bounty of shopping and dining options. In Portland, a neighborhood is your mall and its array of eateries your food court.

Located right on the streetcar line in the Nob Hill shopping district, the Inn at Northrup Station (2025 NW Northrup; 503–224–0543) is simple hip and colorful. And since it's *"in the middle but on the edge,"* this hotel can obviously accommodate as the go to base for the shopping spree select. Therefore, set up camp, freshen up, and hit the ground prowling.

7:00 PM

ABCs OF PORTLAND

The beautiful, Victorian-lined, east-west streets of Nob Hill and northwest Portland are laid out alphabetically, and the north-south streets run numerically. From Northrup where your hotel sits, down 23rd Avenue as well as portions of 21st Avenue, the shopping choices are off the hook between Burnside and Thurman. Check out www.mapclicks.com for an A to Z listing and location map, so your pursuit will have the advantage of a visual on the lay of the land.

At this time of night not everything will be open, but much will, and there will of course be a Friday night hum in the air.

Some standouts:

3 Monkeys (811 NW 23rd Avenue; 503–222–5160) is part estate sale, part high-end boutique. It's "Rock Star Apparel," and it's vintage accoutrements. It's purses strewn up the stairway and monkeys in the window. It's beautiful skirts, blouses, and bags—and garage sale menagerie. Simply, it's an extended stay if you let it.

The Powder Room (814 NW 23rd Avenue; 503–248–9160) offers "Guilt-free shopping," or in other words high fashion at inexpensive prices, on the basement level of one of the adorable storefront houses that Nob Hill is just crazy about. And if you're a hat person, we bid you good luck on making it back through the door without your hair in tried-on disarray. But that's okay. That's what the bazillion hats you just bought are for.

Kiehl's (712 NW 23rd; 503–223–7676) has been providing solutions since 1851 for your hair, face, and body needs. With an extensive product catalog that reads like a menu—complete with ingredients like avocadoes, apricot kernels, and almonds—Kiehl's offers everything to firm, tone, lift, shape, moisturize, and exfoliate.

159

9:00 PM

SEA AND BE SEEN

You're probably ready at this point to show off a bauble or blouse from your new booty. And since you likely revved an appetite by the time you reached K, or Kearney, and/or shops are closing, take a culinary dip in the Mediterranean at Serratto (2112 NW Kearney; 503–221–1195). The energetic yet elegant dining room, which you'll find just two blocks east of 23rd near NW 21st Avenue, is the perfect accompaniment to the mood of this weekend getaway as well as to dishes like the housemade tagliatelle with ragu of wild boar, red wine, and tomatoes or the pork loin with apple compote and coriander spaetzle.

11:00 PM

LOCAL FLAVOR

You've had dinner, maybe even dessert, and now chances are you're even hungrier for more local flavor. Muu-Muu's (612 NW 21st Avenue; 503–223–8169) is a "big world diner," and they're certainly happy to serve you anything from Szechuan to Cajun. But at this time of night you're entering Muu-Muu's for the small world, tight community feel of Portland. It's the kind of place where locals are hanging together clanking beers by afternoon, and they'll likely make you an honorary neighbor long before last call.

SATURDAY

9:00 AM

EGGS IN THE CITY

You're going to be pounding the shopping pavement along NE Broadway in the Irvington District to start your day. Hence that's where all forms of consumption should begin.

Milo's City Café (1325 NE Broadway; 503–288–MILO) offers a metropolitan array of choices with nowhere near a cosmo gouge in prices. The dining area is large, open-kitchen style, so you can sit back and watch like the lifestyle programming voyeur you are while enjoying the sophisticated, urbane offerings such as any one of several different twists on eggs benedict. And with most averaging around $8.00, you can fuel up and still keep the bucks boutique bound.

10:30 AM

BEELINE

The Irvington neighborhood is classified as historic, and, should you feel like a stroll, many of the tree-lined streets are pure Americana to behold. Like many of Portland's neighborhoods, Irvington possesses a commercial core that is eclectic, interesting, and fun. The primary emphasis of retail activity in the neighborhood streams along NE Broadway in a row you never have to veer from between approximately NE 7th to NE 33rd Avenues, and it is definitely worth the walk.

161

Some Standouts:

Goodnight Room (1517 NE Broadway; 503–281–5516) is on a mission to, "make your child's room a dream come true." Serving only the young ones—from babies all the way up to teens—Goodnight Room will furnish their room, decorate it, supply it with unique and educational toys, and much more to make it easier for the little tyke to sleep tight and be ready for the days—and years—ahead.

Oh Baby (1811 NE Broadway; 503–281–7430) means playful naughty and high-end sexy in an award winning lingerie boutique that is "thigh-high in styles, sizes and price range." A bed used to display various articles of nether region attire serves as the centerpiece of an enterprise that does bras—all the way to G—to corsets, buttless slips to thongs, and a few toys thrown in between.

Great Wine Buys (1515 NE Broadway; 503–287–2897) clocks in at over 20 years of business, making it one of the oldest wine retail shops of its kind in the Portland area. A serious wine business with the Portland casual feel, Great Wine Buys lets you enter the wine experience at whatever level makes you comfortable, from accessible to expensive to "geeky." With over 700 wines from around the world, Great Wine Buys also offers classes, Friday night and Saturday tastings, glassware, and even a bridal registry.

1:00 PM

A LOAD OFF

Take a break from the chase and pull up a chair at either

Pour Wine Bar & Bistro (2755 NE Broadway; 503–288–POUR) or Thatch Tiki Bar (2733 NE Broadway; 503–281–8454). Close neighbors and owned by the same person, Pour and Thatch each offer very different options for a possible afternoon libation and snack to get you back on your shopping feet.

Pour is at once minimalist, modern, white-on-white hip and palpably retro, transporting the incoming bibber into a time of key parties and Naugahyde, when words like "groovy" were out of sight, and Bob Newhart and Suzanne Pleshette were weekly icons of fashion. Pour offers daily flights, and their wines by the glass of course include many wineries of the northwest and California, but international choices are incorporated as well. Likewise, the relatively small food menu can pair you up with a dish of mac and cheese or escargot.

Thatch Tiki Bar also transports, this time over the mandatory bridge you have to cross in order to enter the classic tiki atmosphere where you're greeted with bamboo, puffer fish lamps, PuPu platters, and the real Bradys-on-Break deal.

2:30 PM

PHAT ALBERTA

Portland's Alberta Arts District remains a locus of high-charged change. It's morphing at a rate you can almost hear. Many of the area's proprietors are also its neighbors and have a vested stake in making this district work. They are aware of their role as commercial settlers claiming what was once largely commercially forgotten. And they know that success in adventure comes with strength in numbers, so they take care of each other. They are patrons in one another's establishments. And they recommend one another. In Portland's Alberta neighborhood, businesses clustered together mean the opportunity to thrive, not cut throats.

At first glance, the name "Alberta Arts District" may seem a little overstated when taking into account the number of galleries on the street. But when one discovers that nearly every business—from restaurants and bars to the finest in dress shops, with very little exception—functions as a gallery with a rotating roster of artists represented on the walls, one begins to understand the full nature of this community's devotion to art.

And along Alberta you will also find a community devoted to truly distinctive, special, and even, believe it or not, inspiring retail.

Some Standouts:

Foundation Garments (2712 NE Alberta; 503–282–2763) is based, so-to-speak, on the inalienable right of all not to have to toil in unfair or unsafe conditions. To that end, they stock only those brands produced in facilities that meet human rights standards. The owner/operators, a sister and brother-in-law team, research the production facilities themselves and/or limit their inventory to those brands where there is a "connectedness" between the designer and the finished product—meaning, the designer actually hand makes the product, or the designer directly oversees production. In this way, Foundation ensures sweatshop-free merchandise in their store as well as their online sales operation, both of which carry many styles in men's and women's clothing.

Donna & Toots (1631 NE Alberta; 503–241–5570) does fashions from scratch, which means that absolutely everything in their namesake brand is an original pattern and sewn by hand, from scratch on the premises. The designs range from retro innovative to modern fresh, dresses to skirts to tops to hats to more. And since owner/designer/seamstress Suzanne Kraft actually creates her own patterns, she and her apprentices then form the production line.

Named after Suzanne's fashionista, party girl grandmother and great aunt, Donna & Toots also holds sewing classes in their homey showroom and features other clothing and accessory brands as well such as glima t-shirts, Live A Little Sportswear, and Conserve Bags, which makes adorable purses out of recycled plastic bags.

Tribute (1805 NE Alberta; 503–493–9520) and its relatively young proprietors, Josh Beaudry and Andy Westhusing, have landed a different move on Alberta, flying in the face of the notion that skateboarding is a young person's sport but not business. Tribute is the heck-a-cool brand of skateboards and skateboard apparel that they created and were distributing to other outlets for a few years before opening this sole brand retail and distribution operation.

Tumbleweed (1812 NE Alberta; 503–335–3100) began in 2000 when Kara Larson decided to settle down in her hometown of Portland after going so far as to sell her designs out of a suitcase on the road. Once back, she opened her own shop featuring her selection of hand-made, personally designed, one-of-a-kind dresses under the label, Kara-line.

In addition to Kara's draping, romantic dresses, she also carries several other lines from Red Engine jeans to Park Vogel collections. But she's done so well with her own brand and has been so inspired by her young son, that she opened playful children's shop...

...Grasshopper (1816 NE Alberta; 503–335–3131), which sells unique toys and books in addition to the hand-made clothing line that Kara created just for kids called Wild Carrots, covering dresses, tees, and even shoes and socks.

IGPEI (1534 NE Alberta; 503–775–9599) is ig-Pa atin-La for the most uniquely owned toy store you've likely ever entered. Understanding that no one knows toys like a youngster, Beka Amblin, the owner of Origin Flowers which shares the other half of the retail area, began IGPEI with the smartest, most able toy consumer she knew, her 13-year-old son.

In a 50/50 partnership, the son is the sole buyer and is responsible for 100% of his side of the showroom's design. He specializes in small, affordable gifts because he wants every kid in the neighborhood to be able to shop there. His market philosophy mandates that someone his age should be able to walk in with his or her allowance and be able to buy what they want, not just salivate over that unattainable item that requires a birthday to acquisition.

NEED MORE AMMO?

In case the chase has drained more than your pocketbook, or you weren't hungry during the earlier pit stop in Irvington, at any point while in Alberta take a quick and delicious respite at Halibuts (2525 NE Alberta; 503–808–9600). Already an Alberta institution in its short tenure, Halibuts does the best halibut fish and chips bar none. All orders seem to come with a side of smiles in a double-sided establishment where you can choose to go either fish-shack-esque or comfy bar/lounge.

5:00 PM

SHUCK THE PEARL

Like Alberta, Portland's Pearl District is an extreme example of a successful urban makeover, in this case from industrial warehouse grit to industrial warehouse chic—with the addition of modern condo towers, art galleries, fine cuisine, and an adult shopping capital.

Some standouts:

Dress Code (216 NW 13th Avenue; 971–544–0902) fits the uber hip, male Pearl loft dweller like a relaxed pair of imported, Swedish twill chinos. Offering suits to jeans, sweaters to belts, Dress Code travels in international and domestic fashion runway designer circles like J. Lindeberg, Filipa K, Duckie Brown, Hanro, Jack Spade, Allegri, and Oliver Spencer in a showroom that literally glows with minimalist class.

Matisse (1236 NW Flanders; 503–287–5414) is what the owner calls, "Portland's best kept secret." Despite the fact that they never advertise, Matisse has thrived as a ladies' dress shop for all occasions and an alternative wedding boutique.

Part of the reason for their success undoubtedly has to do with the fact that this interesting business absolutely oozes femininity. The proprietor and every single member of her staff are former dancers and are current dance teachers, and much of their clientele consists of dancers. Stepping into the boutique is like walking in on a sexy cabaret changing room where even the walls are French patina chic, and the bodies are chiseled by the discipline and demands of ballet. The dresses are often of European design, several handmade. All are new but many are vintage inspired.

Sole (1033 NW Couch; 503–222–SOLE) began as a small gift shop inside The Heathman Hotel ten years ago. Since then, owner Kim Lane has built an operation that includes a clothing store and a clearance store (The Bee and Thistle and The Bargain Bee respectively) and of course Sole.

As you might imagine, Sole carries shoes, ladies shoes that are unique and not likely to be found anywhere else. And most pairs check in at under $100.00. She also carries handbags and jewelry, the latter running anywhere from $19.00 to $500.00. With prices that typically skew toward reasonable and super friendly service, Sole is one of those places that seems to remember that, though they compete in the trendy and often expensive market that is the Pearl District, they are first and foremost Portland.

Relish (433 NW 10th Avenue; 503–227–3779) is a shopping destination you can share with your friends, men and women, again and again and still see something new. Relish claims that it is "the zone between individuality and mass production." What does that mean? It's "a carefully curated collection of emerging designers from around the globe." It means home décor, textiles, jewelry, handbags, dishes—so unique that much of the stock requires an inquiry with the sales staff as to exactly what the item is and does. And that's when you've gotta have it.

Monique's Boutique (429 NW 10th Avenue; 503–294–0094) caters to the "mature but modern thinking woman" and offers 20 years of experience as well as high-style clothing that is, get this, travel friendly. So most items in the store actually pack well, from dresses to hats, making Monique's Boutique the official retail resource for the Pearl jet set or those just jetting in.

Cargo (380 NW 13th Avenue; 503–209–8349) is simply packed with treasures. Housed in one of the Pearl's many now fashionable warehouses, Cargo offers boatloads of choices literally handpicked from around the globe for your home and garden.

Owner Patty Merrill shops the world over and then imports directly from such regulars as India, Indonesia, Vietnam, China, and the Philippines. Trusted native traders also send inventory her way from Africa, and her gracious staff claims that a new container loaded with different imports arrives every month. So shopping at Cargo with its carved Indonesian gates, Russian icons, rickshaws, paper lanterns, Afghani jewelry, Balinese jewelry, gongs—it's endless—all amazingly well organized in a cavernous, two-story

169

warehouse, is something like arriving at the dock on ship-
ment day and shouldn't be missed.

8:00 PM

A DASH OF PEARL SPICE

In the Pearl District, Oba Restaurante Y Refresqueria de
Lujo (555 NW 12th Avenue; 503–228–6161) translates to
nuevo Latino cuisine with accolades shouting out from local rags all the way to *The New York Times*.

The bar at Oba offers the kind of sizzling atmosphere
where shopping doesn't have to cease, so-to-speak, and
dining is defined by fusion and a little heat right where you
want it. So relax your marching feet, enjoy a glass of wine
from their extensive selection, and partake of such creative
nibbles as a Misty Isle Farms New York steak with cumin-
coriander crust or roasted butternut squash enchiladas.

10:30 PM

CHECK INTO REHAB

You've rested your legs. Now it's time to work the steps—
as you move to the DJ mixes of the Bettie Ford Lounge
(1135 SW Washington; 503–445–8331). An L.A.-esque
club experience complete with celebrity sightings, the Bettie Ford Lounge is glamour and sexiness and, therefore, the
perfect little number with which to accessorize your shopping weekend. And if you happen to have others in tow and
desire an even more exclusive indulgence than may be ex-

perienced at any one of the club's three bars, the Bettie Ford VIP lounge is available by reservation.

SUNDAY

9:00 AM

COURSE OF EXPLORATION

Likely your preference is to save your shopping mojo for the stores and not wear it out on a buffet counter. So, just like this eatery's namesake, Meriwether's Restaurant (2601 NW Vaughn at NW 26th Avenue; 503–228–1250) allows you to chart your own course through such breakfast menu choices as the rustic French toast with rhubarb compote and mascarpone or the local mushroom, gruyere, and Herbes de Provence omelet. You may also map your way to an inside table or enjoy one of Portland's finest patios.

11:00 AM

ABC FOR EFFORT

There is no way you did more than scratch the surface of Nob Hill on your Friday night excursion there, so now's the time to return to finish the alphabet or at least enjoy the attempt.

Some further standouts:

(To be sure, these inclusions are not secondary to the other Nob Hill entries because they are listed later. Many of these businesses simply close earlier and might not have been open on a Friday night.)

Stella's on 21st (1108 NW 21st Avenue; 503–295–5930), as the name implies, definitely tries to distance itself from the competition two blocks away. The explicit intention of owners Robyn Craig and Nancy Goodwin is to be "funkier" than 23rd while trying to keep prices low, ever mindful to maintain the price point at fair. Much of the inventory is local. Some is consignment. And eclectic and colorful are the mandates.

A kitchen sink store (as in everything but), Stella's on 21st sells arbors to art, and there are still twenty-five more letters! So if you're thinking of gifting a special someone upon your return from Portland, Stella's has a wide variety of ideas *and* the card to go with it *and* will wrap for free. It's like the warm feeling you get when batteries are included.

Blake (2285 NW Johnson Street at NW 23rd; 503–222–4848) is Portlandian for denim. At Blake, denim is the focus. Denim is the business. Showcasing 42 different brands of denim in one store, Blake boasts the largest selection in Oregon. And in case you think you've got one of those figures that doesn't contour well in a pair of jeans, might wanna stroll into the store that's got the street rep for being able to denim any derrière.

MammaRo (940 NW 23rd; 503–241–4960) is the sole United States distributor for the Mamma Ro brand of Italian handmade, tabletop ceramics and home accessories. Consequently, as you might imagine, the store on NW 23rd is a dazzling table setting for hundreds. So beautiful is the showroom that its catalog is divided by color. And so extensive is the line of products that there is a category just for rectangular service.

2:00 PM

GIVE IT A REST

At the New Old Lompoc (1616 NW 23rd Avenue; 503–225–1855) they could have had us at beer, but they say hello with reasonably priced, wonderful plates like their own pulled pork and coleslaw sandwich and calamari with three delish sauces. Then they seal the deal on inside flavor by being *the* Red Sox bar in the area, and outside they provide a leafy patio refuge.

So set down your bags, pull up a seat, and enjoy a tasty homemade brew and sandwich. After all, now's the time to rest both you and your wallet while celebrating the valiant, heroic, and wise shopper you've been. There oughta be a trophy.

Important Side Note: If to a mall you must, one of the more exceptional examples to be found is certainly Pioneer Place (700 SW 5th Avenue; 503–228–5800). Located in the very heart of downtown, between the east and westbound trains in fact, Pioneer Place has been built so coherently into its office building and commercial landscape that it is nearly camouflaged. You still get all the mandatory Gap, Guess? and food court charm you can stomach, but this time, instead of sprawling over acres of suburbia, the mall is housed concisely in a few downtown buildings attached by tunnels and an elevated pedestrian bridge.

The Skinny

Lay Your Head

Inn at Northrup Station 2025 NW Northrup; 503–224–0543; www.northrupstation.com

Cool Your Heels

Bettie Ford Lounge 1135 SW Washington; 503–445–8331; www.bettiefordlounge.com
Halibuts 2525 NE Alberta; 503–808–9600
Meriwether's Restaurant 2601 NW Vaughn at NW 26th Avenue; 503–228–1250; www.meriwethersnw.com
Milo's City Café 1325 NE Broadway; 503–288–MILO
Muu–Muu's 612 NW 21st Avenue; 503–223–8169
New Old Lompoc 1616 NW 23rd Avenue; 503–225–1855; www.newoldlompoc.com
Oba Restaurante Y Refresqueria de Lujo 555 NW 12th Avenue; 503–228–6161; www.obarestaurant.com
Pour Wine Bar & Bistro 2755 NE Broadway; 503–288–POUR; www.pourwinebar.com
Serratto 2112 NW Kearney; 503–221–1195; www.serratto.com
Thatch Tiki Bar 2733 NE Broadway; 503–281–8454
Urban Flora 2865 SE Division; 503–236–3344

Get It In Gear

3 Monkeys 811 NW 23rd Avenue; 503–222–5160
Ashiyu 8015 SE 13th Avenue; 503–232–0920;
www.ashiyu.com
Blake 2285 NW Johnson Street at NW 23rd; 503–222–
4848; www.loveblake.com
Cargo 380 NW 13th Avenue; 503–209–8349;
www.cargoinc.com
Donna & Toots 1631 NE Alberta; 503–241–5570;
www.donnaandtoots.com
Dress Code 216 NW 13th Avenue; 971–544–0902;
www.dresscodemensclothing.com
EWF Modern 1122 NW Glisan; 503–295–7336;
www.ewfmodern.com
Foundation Garments 2712 NE Alberta; 503–282–2763;
http://www.foundationgarmentsinc.com/
Goodnight Room 1517 NE Broadway; 503–281–5516;
www.goodnightroom.com
Grasshopper 1816 NE Alberta; 503–335–3131;
www.grasshopperstore.com
Great Wine Buys 1515 NE Broadway; 503–287–2897;
www.greatwinebuys.com
IGPEI 1534 NE Alberta; 503–775–9599
Kiehl's 712 NW 23rd; 503–223–7676; www.kiehls.com
MammaRo 940 NW 23rd; 503–241–4960;
www.mammaro.us
Matisse 1236 NW Flanders; 503–287–5414;
www.matisseboutique.com
Monique's Boutique 429 NW 10th Avenue; 503–294–
0094; www.moniquesboutiqueportland.com
Oh Baby 1811 NE Broadway; 503–281–7430;
www.ohbabyforyou.com

Pioneer Place Mall 700 SW 5th Avenue; 503–228–5800;
www.pioneerplace.com
Powder Room 814 NW 23rd Avenue; 503–248–9160
Relish 433 NW 10th Avenue; 503–227–3779;
www.relishstyle.com
Sole 1033 NW Couch; 503–222–SOLE;
www.4mysole.com
Stella's on 21st 1108 NW 21st Avenue; 503–295–5930;
www.stellason21st.com
Tribute 1805 NE Alberta; 503–493–9520
Tumbleweed 1812 NE Alberta; 503–335–3100;
www.tumbleweedboutique.com

Check Under the 'Hood

Alberta Arts District
www.portlandneighborhood.com/alberta–street.html

Downtown
www.portlandneighborhood.com/downtown–portland.html

Irvington
www.portlandneighborhood.com/irvington.html

Nob Hill
www.portlandneighborhood.com/nobhill.html

Pearl District
www.portlandneighborhood.com/pearldistrict.html

Getting Around Portland

MAX Light Rail Train

A ccessible and navigable are two words that come to mind when you think of Portland. Historically designed to curb urban sprawl, in large part to protect the sanctity of the natural bounty that surrounds us, Portland has been primarily and consciously built up instead of out. Subsequently, the close quarters have no doubt helped to spawn Portland's palpable community feel, and they have also made a viable—and enviable—public transit system a necessity and reality. Several cities far larger than ours can't hold a candle to our mass transit, which is just one more reason why Portland is a metropolitan mecca and yet a comparatively traversable breeze.

So, before you begin your weekend adventures in Portland, acquaint yourself with the transportation options outlined in this chapter and plot your course ahead of time. If you live in Portland, you are probably already aware of just how fabulous and thorough our mass transit system is. Still, some of its features might surprise you. So before you hop in your car, be sure to read this chapter thoroughly for ideas that might save you parking fees, gas money, and any unnecessary headache.

In addition to avoiding the car, you might consider packing the bike as this is one of the most bicycle friendly cities in the entire country. But if that's not convenient, we have also provided information on bike rental.

And finally, nothing beats walking for the best up close and personal perspective of an area. Of course, as an added benefit of biking or walking, the exercise will help to burn off all of those great dining recommendations we lined up for you.

ORIENTEERING

First of all, getting lost in Portland is almost something you have to try to do. Once you're aware of a few of the area's layout basics, disorientation and confusion will just have to be reserved for visiting other cities.

Most importantly, Portland is divided into quadrants. The Willamette River, hard to miss, serves as the natural border between east and west Portland. And, between north and south, the dividing line is Burnside Street. So, for example, if you happen to be standing north of Burnside and east of the river, guess what, you're in Northeast Portland. Elementary. And no matter where you are, the street signs, every one, will tell you which quadrant you're currently occupying. Every address you see will list the coordinates in abbreviated form before the name of the street (ex: 2301 SW Park Avenue). The only exception to any of this is a relatively small area of town that sits east of the Willamette and west of NE Interstate Avenue. This is called North Portland in addition to its rather tongue-in-cheek nickname, the Fifth Quadrant.

TWO LEGS

It is very possible to visit Portland, quite intimately in fact, with nothing more than your walking feet and virtually a toddler's ability to access public transportation. A car isn't a must—even for many who live here—and might prove more hassle than help. So, if you will be primarily hoofing it, the Portland Department of Transportation (PDOT) has a wealth of valuable information to steer you in the right direction. Just visit www.portlandonline.com and follow the

182

links for **Transportation > Maps > Area Walking Maps.** When you click on a selected walking map, be sure to look for the "suggested walking tours" concerning that area for an instant guide. Free walking maps are available for online (PDF format) viewing, or you can order free printed maps.

TWO WHEELS

There are many fantastic Portland biking resources available if you want to explore Portland by cycle. For bike rental information, consult the *Romantic, Active,* and *Nature Weekend* chapters of this book. Also, you may stop in any one of our great bike shops for maps, directions, and personal advice, or visit one of the following biking resources for online maps and more.

Once again, the City of Portland Office of Transportation comes to the rescue with a wealth of online information about how to explore our great city by bicycle. Visit www.portlandonline.com then simply follow the links to **Transportation > Transportation Options > Bicycles.** Just a few of the available resources include bike maps, bike laws, bicycle organizations, tours, summer cycle rides, and more.

Still looking for more biking information? Find a Portland bike route using an online trip planner:

Bycycle.org URL:
http://bycycle.org/

View local bike maps in 3–D. Check out the Metro Bike Map on Google Earth at www.metro–region.org and follow the links to **Transportation > RTP > Bike > Bike Map > Google Earth**.

Metro–Region.org URL:
http://www.metro–region.org/article.cfm?ArticleID=15341

BUS, LIGHT RAIL & STREETCAR

TriMet is the name of Portland's three-pronged attack on traffic congestion. It offers affordable transportation via bus, light rail train (known as the MAX), and streetcar. Taken together, this is a very comprehensive system with extensive crisscrossing of service that means where one transportation method leaves off another should pick right up, getting you to your destination easily.

TriMet's Main Website URL:
www.trimet.org

Biking and Trimet
Want to bring your bicycle on TriMet? Of course you can. Visit the following link to learn more about how to take your bike on the TriMet lines.

TriMet How To Ride URL:
http://www.trimet.org/howtoride/bikes/index.htm

Fareless Square
A large portion of the TriMet route called Fareless Square is offered to riders free of charge. All you have to do is hop on and hop off, no questions asked.

Fareless Square URL:
http://www.trimet.org/fares/fareless.htm

TriMet Trip Planning URL:
http://www.trimet.org/go/cgi–bin/plantrip.cgi

TriMet Maps and Schedules URL:
http://www.trimet.org/schedules/index.htm

TriMet to Popular Destinations URL:
http://www.trimet.org/find/index.htm

TAXI, SEDAN & SHUTTLE SERVICES

Radio Cab
(503) 227–1212
www.radiocab.net

Broadway Cab
(503) 227–1234
www.broadwaycab.com

Prime Towncar (sedan)
(503) 653-0500
www.home.comcast.net/~primeag

Green Shuttle
(503) 252–4422
www.greentrans.com

Blue Star Airporter (shuttle)
(503) 249–1837
www.bluestarbus.com

UNIQUE RIDES

If you're looking for a ride that is a little out of the ordinary, Portland's got those too.

Portland Aerial Tram
Enjoy stunning views while suspended 500 feet in the air for a 3-minute voyage from Portland's South Waterfront up Marquam Hill to OHSU (Oregon Health Sciences University).

Portland Aerial Tram Home Page URL:
http://www.portlandtram.org/

Horse Drawn Carriage Rides
Golden Times Carriage Service (503–666–4647) will pick you up and treat you to a one of a kind ride for a half-hour, hour, or longer.

Pedicab
Relax and enjoy a tour in the Portland Metro area in an environmentally sound, human-powered vehicle that is a modern take on the rickshaw.

Portland Rose Pedals Pedicab
503–421–7433
http://www.rosepedals.com

PDX Pedicab
503–733–4222
http://www.pdxpedicab.com

MORE PORTLAND TRANSPORTATION RE-SOURCES

And of course, visit the "Getting Around" page on our own **PortlandNeighborhood.com** for more ideas, including helpful links to Portland gas prices and more.

PortlandNeighborhood Getting Around URL:
http://www.portlandneighborhood.com/transportation.html

Index

About the Authors

We are longtime Portland locals on a mission: to enjoy and promote our Portland neighborhoods and the independent businesses, artists, and neighbors who thrive in them.

Dana Speer has worked as a fulltime film and television writer for ten years. When Dana arrived here from her home in Long Beach, California, she found herself suddenly in a passionate panic to uncover it all. That moment, there and then, she began exploring this city of roses, this city of bridges, this city of beer, this city of smiles. She didn't comb the streets. She scoured them, over and over, back and forth, as many as she could lay her feet on. The problem was, however, she had nowhere near enough people to tell about the treasure she was unearthing like some cosmopolitan anthropologist. Then she found Portland-Neighborhood.com and two women of like mind who had been infected with Portland in exactly the same way. Now, lucky her, Dana finds that, via the website and works like *PortlandNeighborhood's Guide to the Perfect Portland Weekend*, she is engaged in a dialogue with an entire city, a city she dearly loves and a city whose story she desperately wants to learn and share.

Lorri Ely founded PortlandNeighborhood.com after moving to Portland from the Midwest and falling in love with the Pacific Northwest and the city of Portland. Each Portland neighborhood seemed to have its own unique personality, so the website was designed with a neighborhood perspective in mind. Responding to website emails from Portlanders and visitors prompted the idea for a unique Portland travel book. People seemed to be thirsting for more ideas on what was the best thing to see and do in Portland. It seemed like the uniqueness of Portland deserved more than a boring travel guide with a simple list of places to go. Many of the ideas in this book are simply a result of a love affair with Portland; as Lorri explores the city she continues to discover more wonderful things to see and do, and thus many of the seeds of ideas for *perfect weekends* were planted.

Angela Scott is a co-founder of PortlandNeighborhood.com and shares a passion for this wonderful city. A decade long resident of Portland, and originally from Iowa, Angela escaped the endless sea of corn fields and made the 1700 mile hop to Portland seemingly on a whim. The truth is, a consulting gig and a deep desire to eat something other than meat and 'taties was well worth the risk of landing in a new city sight unseen. "After one look, I knew it: I'll never leave," she said. The truth is, after discovering Portland you couldn't have convinced her there was another place in the world she was more suited for. Exploring Portland is a passion, and many of Angela's personal favorite Portland haunts appear throughout this book.